UE

Boswell's Johnson

Boswell's Johnson

A Preface to the
Life

RICHARD B. SCHWARTZ

The University of Wisconsin Press

Published 1978

The University of Wisconsin Press
Box 1379, Madison, Wisconsin 53701

The University of Wisconsin Press, Ltd.
70 Great Russell Street, London

Copyright © 1978
The Board of Regents of the University of Wisconsin System

First printing

Printed in the United States of America
For LC CIP information see the colophon

ISBN 0-299-07630-X

FOR
Judith and Jonathan

Contents

Acknowledgments

This study was completed with the aid of three research grants, two from the Graduate School and one from the Institute for Research in the Humanities at the University of Wisconsin, Madison. It is a pleasure to record my thanks for those awards and for the help of Loretta Freiling and Robert Kingdon at the Humanities Institute. A number of individuals have provided help and support of various kinds: Robert M. Bock, James L. Clifford, Larry L. Cummings, Barbara Hughes Fowler, Donald Greene, Robert L. Haig, Ian Loram, Frank D. McConnell, and Eric Rude. The mention of their names here does not begin to express my appreciation for their aid. The staff of the University of Wisconsin Press has, as always, been both expert and cooperative. Chapter V of this study is a revised and expanded version of material that originally appeared in *Genre;* my thanks are due to the editor of that journal for permission to reprint. Finally, I would thank my wife Judith and son Jonathan, whose interest is exceeded only by their support and whose support has never been exceeded.

Madison, Wisconsin   R.B.S.
September 1977

Introduction

My chief purpose in this study is to treat those contexts which best elucidate the nature of Boswell's achievement in his biography of Johnson. I begin with theories of life-writing and argue that—with certain adjustments— modern discussions of biography and autobiography are more useful than the theoretical commentary of Boswell's predecessors and contemporaries. Boswell's implicit theory of biography is quasi-scientific; it is, accordingly, discussed in the context of eighteenth-century scientific methodology in chapter II. The *Life* is one of the great accomplishments in that body of eighteenth-century literature which treats historical realities through the use of literary devices. Such literature often involves a consideration of the relationship between those realities and the writer's artifices. The treatment of that relationship, both in Boswell and in the works of other major eighteenth-century figures, follows a roughly discernible pattern which finds analogies in eighteenth-century epistemology. The crucial aspect of that pattern is control, an element treated in the contexts of the London Journal and the *Life*. The "scientific analogy" of chapter II deals with the overall structure of the *Life*, the "epistemological analogy" of chapter III with individual "scenes" or sections within the *Life*.

The fourth chapter raises the seldom discussed issue of setting within the *Life*. The notion is to be interpreted broadly. Some applications are specific but my chief concern is the type of context in which Boswell presents his biographical subject. One of my major criticisms of Boswell is the limited stress which he places on the importance of biographical "image," that coherent sense of the biographical subject which emerges from the available material during the process of research and is then used as a basis for organization, shaping, and the selection of details during the process of composition. Boswell's sense of Johnson is too superficial and overlooks (along with much modern scholarship) Johnson's Johnson, the image which emerges in the self-portraits sprinkled throughout Johnson's works, an image discussed in chapter V. The final chapter addresses the question of use. Given my views of the *Life*, to what uses should the book be (or not be) put?

I have purposely avoided a consideration of issues which are ably discussed elsewhere: for example, text, contemporary reception of the *Life*, process of composition, competing contemporary biographies of Johnson. My study is prefatory rather than exhaustive. I assume a dynamic relationship between evidence and evaluation, that is, each bit of new evidence concerning Johnson alters (in some fashion) our sense of Boswell's *Life*. Boswell should be judged, ultimately, on his sense of Johnson's personality and thought, but that norm supposes an objective sense of Johnson against which Boswell's can be measured. Because the "objective" Johnson is based on constantly growing evidence and is thus never static, a "final," exhaustive judgment of Boswell is impossible. It is thus of far greater importance to establish the kinds of contexts in which such a judgment will occur. Hence the nature of my study.

Modern scholarship has tended to separate the two crucial facets of the life-writer's work: the gathering of his facts and the shaping of those facts. Boswell prided himself upon the former; his modern admirers often focus upon the latter. One of my interests concerns the inseparability of these two activities. In the process of my discussion, some sense of modern Boswell scholarship should emerge. I do not intend any sort of summary or survey of that commentary but do wish to indicate the fact that the structure of the commentary often elucidates theoretical issues.

Numerous studies of the *Life* or sections of the *Life* have appeared in recent years. The studies whose interests most closely parallel my own are William Siebenschuh's; our conclusions, however, are quite different. I share the current admiration for Boswell's craft (justified most ably, I think, by Ralph Rader and Paul Alkon) but I consider it somewhat exaggerated. Similarly, I accept the majority of the complaints lodged against the *Life* (preeminently by Donald Greene) but am not persuaded that they diminish the greatness of Boswell's book. What concerns me are the possible uses of that book once its shortcomings as biography are acknowledged. In my own discussion I have presupposed a basic awareness of the interests and arguments of contemporary Boswell scholarship.

I have attempted to eliminate annotation whenever possible. All references within the text are given in complete form in the bibliography; key primary works are referred to in abbreviated form, the abbreviations appearing at the beginning of the bibliography. The bibliography is selective. There is no pretense here concerning completeness. Most major studies of the *Life* are included, but the primary purpose of the bibliography is to eliminate the need for annotation and to convey a sense of the kind of reading on which my study is based.

I would add a final note. It will perhaps be assumed that my criticism of Boswell is severe, my praise damningly faint. Here I will only say what I say throughout the study. The *Life's* importance necessitates searching criticism. Its uses have often been improper ones. To discourage those uses the book's limitations must be stressed. My ultimate purposes are positive: to encourage a greater understanding of Johnson and to suggest uses of Boswell's *Life* which are commensurate with the nature of the book. A realization of Boswell's limitations prepares the way for an investigation of his strengths, while a continual reaffirmation of strengths which are not demonstrable diverts us from the appreciation of his real accomplishments.

Boswell's Johnson

CHAPTER I

The Life-Writer's Task

*I told him [Lord Kames] that I should like much to be
distinguished in that way [as an author], that I was sure that I
had genius, and was not deficient in easiness of expression; but
was at a loss for something to say, and, when I set myself
seriously to think of writing, that I wanted a Subject. (PP, I, 101)*

Early in the *Life* Boswell refers to both *Rambler* 60 and
Idler 84, the papers in which Johnson articulates his
biographical theory and declares his preference for autobiography. In writing the life "of him who excelled all mankind in writing the lives of others" Boswell has usually been
seen as the greatest of biographers, the biographer who,
moreover, follows the "pattern" or "formula" established by
Johnson. Anthony Tillinghast writes that Boswell "worked from
Johnson's example"; "whatever he added, he left nothing of the
Johnsonian formula out" ("The Moral and Philosophical Basis of
Johnson's and Boswell's Idea of Biography," pp. 120-21). Well
into the nineteenth century Boswell and Johnson remained twin
biographical fulcra. Johnson's theoretical pronouncements
represented the culmination of Renaissance and eighteenth-
century commentary, a distillation and consolidation of
cherished principles to which nearly all subscribed; Boswell had
written the greatest of biographies, a study of the figure viewed

simultaneously as both master theoretician and (before Boswell) master practitioner of life-writing.

Johnson's principles may be summarized briefly. As in his treatment of other genres, Johnson is concerned with the possibility of empathy between reader and subject. He is equally convinced of the necessity of close contact between subject and author. The material presented by that author should be relevant to the audience's needs and interests and Johnson places a premium on domestic material for he considers it particularly useful in this regard. Biographical material should be of hortatory value; the reader should be delighted but also instructed by it. The relationship between individual and common human experience—the manner in which each life recapitulates the human pattern—should be traced. In Johnson's judgment "dramatic" material is often, in reality, mundane; large public events are remote from most readers and those readers will respond to such events in the way that they respond to episodes in fairy tales and romances.

Unfortunately, in Johnson's judgment, there is little good biography, a situation partly explained by the number of problems which the biographer confronts. Material which should be preserved is often evanescent. The biographer is tempted to slant those materials which do survive and is forced to decide what to do with unpleasant material that may affect the living—the problem of what is now being termed biographical decorum. Ultimately autobiography is preferable to biography. Only the autobiographer has the facts and the temptation to manipulate those facts in self-serving fashion is so obvious that the autobiographer is able to consciously guard against it. (Few are as sanguine as Johnson in this regard.) Finally, with his century Johnson seldom distinguishes between biography and autobiography; hence the appropriateness of a more general term such as "life-writing."

None of these principles is really unique. They had already appeared in the works of such figures as Bacon, Burnet, Aubrey, Sprat, Dryden, Addison, and Conyers Middleton. Roger North's unpublished comments closely anticipate Johnson's, although North's predate Johnson's by several decades. The single exception, perhaps, is the notion of empathy, important for Coleridge and James Field Stanfield (author of the first real book on biography—1813), but seldom mentioned before Johnson in the context of life-writing. However, the importance of the notion in eighteenth-century epistemology and ethical theory neutralizes any claim of true uniqueness.

Johnson's principles (they were associated with him far more than with his predecessors) pose one major problem: they do little to elucidate his own biographical practices. It should be noted, however, that much of his biographical work is directly affected by external constrictions (for example, the *Gentleman's Magazine* or *Medicinal Dictionary* biographical sketches); it would be both inappropriate and unfair to consider such work within the context of Johnsonian theory and subject it to rigorous inspection. Nevertheless, the single work which is commonly described as best exemplifying his theories is the *Life of Savage*, and there the theory/practice application involves considerable wrenching, for the enormity and uniqueness of Savage's situation stretches such principles as empathy, relevance, and uniformity of experience to extremes. Few of us, fortunately, are tried for murder, imprisoned for debt, and blessed with mothers like the Countess of Macclesfield, a woman whose acts, in Johnson's judgment, are so wicked as to defy interpretation.

Probably the chief attraction of the *Life of Savage* for those seeking a theory/practice parallel is the fact that Johnson personally knew his biographical subject, "for nobody can write the life of a man, but those who have eat and drunk and lived in social intercourse with him" (*Life,* II, 166), but how important, one might ask, is this contact when Johnson relied on published sources for part of the biography and confused many of the facts of Savage's life? The *Life of Savage* is clearly deserving of the praise and attention it has received but it has often been praised for the wrong reasons—reasons based on an attempt to apply Johnsonian principles to Johnsonian practice. What does deserve attention is Johnson's analysis of Savage's character, that facet of Johnson's work which has also been singled out for praise in Johnson's lives of individuals whom he did not know personally.

What is striking about the *Life of Savage* is the extent to which Johnson can elucidate the life and character of his subject while fumbling with his materials. Clarence Tracy, who does understand the facts of Savage's life (to the extent that they may be understood), comments on the overall faithfulness and perspicuity of Johnson's biography:

Johnson seems to be at his best when he has no particular facts at all to go upon, when he pushes his notes aside and allows himself to generalize out of the wealth of his experience and understanding. . . . After considerable study of Savage's career and character from all the available evidence I keep coming back to Johnson for a fairer and clearer view of the man than I can get elsewhere. Johnson, of course, did not know all the facts. . . . ("Johnson and the Art of Anecdote," pp. 91-92)

The implication here is that the understanding of the biographical subject need not be based on a precise use of facts or a herculean accumulation of them. The point is an important one, for Johnson's deft and telling assessments of personality and character sharply distinguish his biographical practices from those of Boswell. In neither case is the framework of eighteenth-century biographical theory particularly useful. The differing tendencies represented by Johnson and Boswell are more the subject of late nineteenth- and twentieth-century theorizing, though such theorizing was, of course, anticipated by eighteenth-century practice and certain facets of eighteenth-century ideology. The ideology in question, however, is more scientific and philosophic than literary. Within the age of Johnson there is a very real correlation between theory and biographical practice but the theory is to be sought in the period's epistemology and science rather than in its commentary on life-writing. Twentieth-century biographical concerns have, in many ways, been generated by nonliterary aspects of seventeenth- and eighteenth-century thought. Thus it is appropriate to treat older practice in the context of later theory, particularly when that later theory is adjusted so as to accord with the complexities of the thought which generated it. It is against the framework of modern biographical theory and eighteenth-century scientific and epistemological theory that one may best assess the norms and achievements of Boswell's *Life*.

The uniformity of late nineteenth- and early twentieth-century comments on life-writing is striking. Terminology changes, but the interests are nearly always the same. There is the continuing concern over the nature of factual evidence and its uses and a realization of the biographer's limitations (versus the novelist's freedom), but the primary interest of modern theorizing is the long overdue realization that biography is an art and should be discussed as such. In more recent years we have been concerned with generic distinctions and have attempted to develop a vocabulary which would enable us to discriminate among the varied forms ("journals," "memoirs," "diaries," "autobiographies," "sketches," for example) which we encounter. In both early and mid-twentieth-century theorizing, however, one is struck by the fact that two generic categories continue to appear. The names change, but the thrust of the distinction is clear:

All biography is obviously and naturally divided into two kinds. There is the biography pure and simple, in which the whole of the materials is passed through the alembic of the biographer, and in which few if any of these materials appear except in an altered and digested condition. This, though apparently the oldest, is artistically the most perfect kind.

[Second, there] is the kind of "applied" or "mixed" biography, including letters from and to the hero, anecdotes about him, and the like, connected and wrought into a whole by narrative and comment of the author. . . . To this belong[s]. . . . Boswell's *Johnson*. . . .

George Saintsbury[1]

The art of biography seems to have fallen on evil times in England. We have had, it is true, a few masterpieces, but we have never had, like the French, a great biographical tradition; we have had no Fontenelles and Condorcets, with their incomparable *éloges*, compressing into a few shining pages the manifold existences of men. . . .

Those two fat volumes, with which it is our custom to commemorate the dead—who does not know them, with their ill-digested masses of

---

1. James L. Clifford, ed., *Biography as an Art*, p. 103. All subsequent references are to this excellent collection.

material, their slipshod style, their tone of tedious panegyric, their lamentable lack of selection, of detachment, of design?

Lytton Strachey (p. 122)

The portraitist takes his basic material from the purely scientific biographer and is always indebted to him. With a kind of naive cynicism, he appropriates the scientist's laboriously collated facts for purposes of his own: an artist who ransacks the flowerbeds and leaves a pillaged garden behind for the grumbling gardener, while he himself goes off with a superb bouquet gleaming in his arms.

Emil Ludwig (p. 136)

In fact two types of biography are conceivable: the work of art in which, of course, facts must be respected, but which admits of legitimate suppressions made for the sake of proportion or composition; and the scholarly biography, in which form is deliberately sacrificed to complete information, and where, therefore, suppression of facts for aesthetical reasons would not be justified.

André Maurois (p. 168)

The function of the historian is akin to that of the painter and not of the photographic camera: to discover and set forth, to single out and stress that which is of the nature of the thing, and not to reproduce indiscriminately all that meets the eye. To distinguish a tree you look at its shape, its bark and leaf; counting and measuring its branches would get you nowhere. Similarly what matters in history is the great outline and the significant detail; what must be avoided is the deadly morass of irrelevant narrative.

Sir Lewis Namier (p. 187)

In short, the life-writer's business is twofold: to gather facts (a quasi-scientific enterprise) and to shape facts (an artistic enterprise). The extent to which one activity is subordinate to the other will determine the type of biography which the life-writer produces, either the "artistic" biography, characterized by insight, brevity, and the judicious use of key details, or the "scientific," scholarly biography which attempts to assemble every possible detail, a work in which the process of accumulation is of greater importance than the process of selection. This distinction is initially useful but ultimately simplistic. It enables us to trace rough generic lines and aids in the general definition of the problem. It also, however, implies that a distinction between accumulation and shaping is really possible, that there are irreducible facts which can be presented "objectively." C. V. Wedgwood appropriately comments that "any way of thinking about, or looking at, historical facts, which has any value at all, must be an exercise of the imaginative and discriminating faculties; History in any intelligible form is *art*" (*Biography as an Art*, p. 217). There may be printed documents which attempt some sort of objectivity (telephone directories, army field manuals detailing the functioning of equipment) but these are very distant from the product of the biographer's labors. He is to produce a work which is intended somehow to suggest, approximate, or represent a human life. He works with "objective" documents but the successful use of such documents (wills, library sale catalogues, inventories of personal property, travel itineraries) turns on the biographer's intelligence and imagination.

With the aid of such excellent studies as Olney's *Metaphors of Self* we have become increasingly aware of the manner in which subjectivist epistemology, particularly eighteenth-century epistemology, bears on life-writing. The stress of biographical shaping (Johnson's forte) now exceeds that of data collection (Boswell's forte). Biography and autobiography cannot hope to faithfully record or reproduce human experience; they can only offer some sort of similitude for that experience. Thus Jung begins his *Memories, Dreams, Reflections* by stating that he hopes to tell his personal myth, his fable. Philip Toynbee discusses the process from the point of view of the reader:

Think for a moment, of the most renowned biography in our language—of Boswell's *Life of Johnson*. As we read that book we transmute what we are reading into the steadily solidifying image of a real man—but always into an image, never into a man. And an image is almost as unlike a man as is a book itself; in fact a book, the physical object, can at least be seen, felt, smelt and tasted like a man, while none of these things can be done to an image. For one thing Boswell's Johnson has a beginning and an end. There are many pages in between them, but even if there were a million more this figure would still be constricted as the real Johnson was never constricted. True the real Johnson was born and he died, but at every second of his life he was, as we all are, infinite, unseizable, imponderable. He had no edges. (*Biography as an Art*, p. 196)

Toynbee's remarks must be supplemented with the comment
that that "image" which emerges is the responsibility of the
biographer rather than his reader. The biographer cannot ab-
dicate this responsibility by presenting material randomly.
Selection of pertinent material is based on an "image" which
emerges from a consideration of all available material. The
selected material is then presented in such a way that the reader
may grasp the "image" without inspecting all possible material,
that is, without taking on the task of the biographer. These then
are my chief concerns in this study: the Boswellian conception of
gathering/shaping, the image of Johnson which emerges (or fails
to emerge) in the *Life*, the relationship between facts and image,
and the possibility of a Johnsonian alternative, an image
emerging from autobiography and self-portraiture whose
usefulness may exceed that of Boswell's. Moreover, the
gathering/shaping dichotomy presents us with a very old
pattern, the distinction (call it what you will) between "objective" fact and subjective apprehension and presentation, the
distinction between "reality" and artifice, a distinction which
eighteenth-century writers undercut with considerable success.
The gathering/shaping process—the creation of an "image" of
the subject—is analogous to key patterns in eighteenth-century
scientific methodology, while the blurring of the line between
the "real" and the artificial is best approached in the context of
eighteenth-century epistemology. The first analogy provides an
entrée into the larger architectonics of Boswell's *Life;* the second
provides a vocabulary for treating individual scenes within the
biography.

As I suggested above, Johnson's biographical practices differ
from Boswell's in ways that point up the initial validity of the
distinction between "artistic" and "scientific" biography. Tracy
praises Johnson's sense of "Savage," his essential understanding
of the man and his ability to provide an image of the man,
despite the awkward handling of facts and chronology. Johnson's "Savage" is remarkably accurate. In 1785 Thomas Tyers
praised Johnson in similar fashion:

His Lives of the Poets (like all his biographical pieces) are well written.
He gives us the pulp without the husks. . . . His perspicacity was very

extraordinary. He was able to take measure of every intellectual object; and to see all round it. If he chose to plume himself as an author, he might on account of the gift of intuition. (Brack and Kelley, eds., *The Early Biographies of Johnson,* pp. 82-83)

In short, Johnson could grasp the nature of his biographical subject and produce a coherent sense of that subject for his reader. His details are often drawn from secondary sources and they are sometimes sparse, but Johnson's grasp of the material that he does have is most impressive. What Tyers does not dwell on is the fact that the life-writer's sense of his subject affects the selection of his material. In the finished book, the image emerges for the reader through the life-writer's judicious use of detail; during the process of composition the details to be used are chosen on the basis of that image. Thus there is an ongoing interaction between the facts which determine the image and the sense of the subject which determines the use of facts—both in the assembling of the materials and in the writing of the life. If the biographer lacks a clear and sophisticated image of his subject he has no proper basis for shaping his materials. His presentation of them is likely to be characterized by chaos or utter blandness. If he has an image or sense of his subject which is "incorrect," which does not square with the totality of the available evidence, it is likely that his materials will be twisted and manipulated in improper fashion. Thus, the biographer's fundamental comprehension of the personality and character of the figure he treats is of inestimable importance. Of course, it is absurd to require a definitive, final explanation which is and always will be closed to challenge. What the reader can require is thoughtful consideration of the available evidence and attention to the multiple facets of the individual personality.

Geoffrey Scott discusses the relationship between details and "image" in the *Life.* His conclusions may be disputed but not his awareness of the precise nature of the issue. He is here comparing Johnson to a kind of genie:

When we examine the book from which this urgent figure is risen, we find a close mosaic of small separate facts and sayings. No biography was ever so free from generality; there is no attempt to explain the secret, to forestall the shape that will form itself on the air; scarcely any propounding and summing; all is particular. Boswell weighs out each tested fragment; and the speck of radium inhering in each generates the energy by which the great total, Johnson, strides on among the living. (*PP*, VI, 15)

Scott comments that "Boswell's conscious effort seems to be fixed far less upon art than upon authenticity" (p. 15), a correct statement, but one that may seem a bit curious in light of the recent attention accorded Boswell's art in the *Life*. Marshall Waingrow acknowledges Scott's remark concerning Boswell's concern for authenticity and adds:

[Boswell] may not have recognized—at least he did not articulate—the double standard in literary biography that perplexes the criticism (without inhibiting the practice) of that *genre;* namely, the competition of so-called scientific and aesthetic requirements. (*Corr—Life*, p. xxv)

Nearly all of Boswell's comments on his own work refer to his reliability and to the authenticity of his materials; nearly all of his recent admirers have been concerned with his art—the shaping of his material—particularly within discrete scenes but also within the larger pattern of the book's structure. I am struck by the ease with which "scientific" and aesthetic requirements are often separated. Tracy's formulation is pertinent:

Boswell . . ., departing radically from these precedents [the "neoclassic" concern with generality], set out to give the world, not a portrait of Johnson in the grand manner of Reynolds, but rather a vast accumulation of detailed fact and anecdote. His reader is not told in a few highly condensed, well-pondered sentences what the essence of Johnson's soul was, but he is asked to follow his life through many pages to listen to his talk, to observe him repeatedly under different circumstances, to draw inferences and make deductions, and to verify and revise every conclusion in the light of later observations. In Boswell's references to his method and achievements in his introduction and letters he valued himself most on the quantity of reliable information he presented, rather than on the finality of his interpretation. . . . ("Johnson and the Art of Anecdote," pp. 86-87)

Leaving aside the possibility of a "final" interpretation of Johnson, one must surely have some coherent and suitably complex sense of Johnson if one is to write his life. The "vast accumulation of detailed fact and anecdote" is a tiny portion of Johnson's life and experience. We are somehow lulled by the length of the *Life* because we compare it with the kind of brief treatments praised by Strachey, but the *Life* is only comparatively long. It can be read in a few days; Johnson lived 75 years. It recounts detailed information but Boswell was only in Johnson's company, by Collins' estimate, for 425 days, and much of that time was spent in the Hebridean tour. The material in the *Life* is highly selective considering the breadth of experience with which the hypothetically ideal biographer might deal.

Our ideal biographer would base his "image" on a consideration of all available evidence, then present to the reader only as much of that evidence as is necessary to create a similitude for Johnson's life which would faithfully represent the breadth and complexity of Johnson's experience. In the case of a biographical subject which involves very little evidence a reader might be content with a bland presentation of that available evidence by a "biographer" whose role is actually editorial. In a sense, however, this is Boswell's posture. He argues that he has offered so much that the reader may easily draw his own conclusions concerning Johnson. I would argue that this will not do in the case of a figure like Johnson who presents such rich and complex material for the biographer to assimilate and shape. The role of shaper cannot be passed on to the reader for the material with which he should, ideally, deal is so vast as to make the *Life* look like a pamphlet. The modern student of Johnson must work through a great deal of material in order to even begin to understand Johnson, much less to write his life: dozens of biographies, reminiscences, and biographical sketches, volumes of correspondence, Johnson's multivolumed (and still uncertain) canon, itself replete with self-portraiture and autobiography, documents such as the library sale catalogue, classic studies of Johnson from the nineteenth and early twentieth centuries, some twenty-five or thirty postwar monographs and at least two hundred articles from the thousands in print. Still, the impressive accomplishments of Johnson's students do not intimidate, for much remains to be said and done. A context such as this dwarfs the material presented in the *Life*. I am not suggesting that Boswell be criticized for not doing the work which it has taken hundreds of scholars to accomplish. Boswell is open to criticism, however, for conveying the impression that he has provided sufficient material for his reader to form a sophisticated sense of Johnson. He has not.

In the case of the *Life* the tendency to separate "scientific" biographical demands from "aesthetic" ones begins with Boswell himself, whose claims are nearly always one-sided:

The labour and anxious attention with which I have collected and arranged [suggesting a neutral, "objective" activity] *the materials . . . will hardly be conceived. . . . (Life,* I, 5-6)

a scrupulous authenticity (Life, I, 6-7)

for perfect authenticity, I . . . (*Life*, III, 358)

I am very exact in authenticity. (*Life*, IV, 83)

that anxious desire of authenticity which prompts a person who is to record conversations. . . . (*Life*, IV, 343)

I beg leave to doubt [Mrs. Piozzi's] perfect authenticity. . . . (*Life*, IV, 346)

a few circumstances, on the authenticity of which [my readers] may perfectly rely. . . . (*Life*, IV, 399)

In every narrative . . . authenticity is of the utmost consequence. (*Tour*, V, 1)

the scrupulous fidelity of my Journal. (*Tour*, V, 279)

that authentick Precision which alone can render Biography valuable. (*Corr—Life*, p. lix)

No doubt Boswell intends multiple meanings of *authentic* (authoritative, reliable, trustworthy, original, firsthand, real, genuine). What is most striking, however, is the leap from authenticity to completeness:

He will be seen . . . more completely than any man who has ever yet lived. (*Life*, I, 30)

it will exhibit him more completely than any person . . . has yet been preserved. . . . (*Corr—Life*, p. 279)

And from relative completeness to near or actual perfection:

I am anxious to make it as perfect as I possibly can. . . . (*Corr—Life*, p. 75)

It appears to me that mine is the best plan of Biography that can be conceived. . . . (*Corr—Life*, p. 265)

I am absolutely certain that *my* mode of Biography . . . is the most perfect that can be conceived. . . . (*Corr—Life*, p. 267)

"Certainty," "completeness," "authenticity," and "perfection" are words which are not used lightly today, and it is fair to question Boswell's use of them, for it is the science and epistemology of the eighteenth century which have caused our circumspection and caution in these regards. These issues were argued at length in Boswell's century and it is thus not inappropriate to treat his theoretical orientation in relation to analogous patterns of eighteenth-century thought.

Even if Boswell's "theory of biography" resists detailed articulation (as some would argue), his own sense of his orientation is unmistakable. He is a scientific biographer with enormous energy and tenacity. He seeks out facts and guarantees their validity. His introduction of certain materials (conversations, private correspondence) is revolutionary both in manner and in extent. He will be a primary source as much (or more) than a secondary one; the *Life* will be a repository of invaluable material. The shaping of that material—that for which he is now so often praised—he mentions infrequently. He appears unconscious of the problems generated by the assumption that the gathering process may be separated from the shaping process.

Boswell uses several metaphors to describe his work. He speaks of his book as a "monument," "an Egyptian Pyramid in which there will be a compleat mummy of Johnson that Literary Monarch" (*Corr—Life*, p. 96); it is his "design in writing the Life of that Great and Good Man, to put as it were into a Mausoleum all of his precious remains that I can gather" (*Corr—Life*, pp. 111-12). Paul Alkon notes that Boswell's references to "preservation" suggest, through submerged metaphor, the biographer's role as that of a kind of embalmer ("Boswellian

Time," p. 244). One metaphor is particularly important. In the *Life* Boswell writes of "the Flemish picture which I give of my friend" (*Life*, III, 191), his interest lying in what he terms "the most minute particulars." In his journal he writes in similar fashion:

I am so nice in recording him that every trifle must be authentic. I draw him in the style of a Flemish painter. I am not satisfied with hitting the large features. I must be exact as to every hair, or even every spot on his countenance. (*Boswell: The Ominous Years*, p. 103)

Pottle considers this a happy comparison and properly associates a "Flemish picture" with "minuteness of graphic depiction" ("James Boswell, Journalist," p. 23). Irma Lustig writes that Boswell is "characterizing by an apt comparison the sharp but minute and literal details by which an artist might recreate reality" ("Boswell's Portrait of Himself in *The Life of Samuel Johnson*," p. 152). In some ways the metaphor is quite surprising for it could easily associate Boswell with Smollett's Pallet in *Peregrine Pickle*, the vain artist whose interest in minuteness is vigorously satirized:

They were conducted by their domestique to the house of a painter, where they found a beggar standing for his picture, and the artist actually employed in representing a huge louse that crawled upon his shoulder. Pallet was wonderfully pleased with this circumstance, which he said was altogether a new thought, and an excellent hint, of which he would make his advantage: and in the course of his survey of this Fleming's performances, perceiving a piece in which two flies were engaged upon the carcase of a dog half devoured, he ran to his brother brush, and swore he was worthy of being a fellow-citizen of the immortal Rubens. . . . He now professed himself more than ever enamoured of the Flemish school. . . .[2]

Boswell risks a great deal in leaving such an opening for the hostile critic. Smollett satirizes the concern with the utterly

---

2. *The Adventures of Peregrine Pickle*, pp. 335-36. Hogarth has been suggested as a possible original for Pallet. For arguments pro and con, see Clifford, pp. 787-88; Ronald Paulson, *Hogarth: His Life, Art, and Times*, II, 133.

trivial and distasteful detail at the expense of beauty and general truth. Moreover, Pallet claims that

in execution he had equalled, if not excelled, the two ancient painters who vied with each other in the representation of a curtain and a bunch of grapes; for he had exhibited the image of a certain object so like to nature, that the bare sight of it set a whole hogsty in an uproar. (p. 335)

Pallet's successes in achieving *enargeia*[3] probably do not rival Zeuxis'; at least his audience is meaner. Smollett's point is that what purports to be absolutely realistic and absolutely lifelike may be accompanied by silliness or huxterism. In short, minute detail may involve the portraitist with the trivial and cause him to lose sight of the important. It may encourage him to claim a kind of realism and faithfulness whose only value is that of a curiosity.

I am not labelling Boswell a biographical Pallet, only suggesting that the norms to which he points are not neutral ones and could easily be turned against him. The test, here and elsewhere, concerns Boswell's consciousness of the slippery nature of his norms and his ability to avoid the problems generated by them while capitalizing on the strategies and advantages associated with them. A scientific analogy is pertinent here. The assembly of data is of crucial importance to the eighteenth-century scientist, but the blind, unsystematic collection of data is an equally important danger, one pointed to by Bacon and enunciated by nearly all of his ideological successors. Data are useful in relation to principles, just as biographical details are useful in relation to the biographer's overarching conception of his subject. The scientist's data and principles, like the biographer's details and "image," are not neatly separable. Their relationship is one of dynamic interaction.

Writing to Hugh Blair in 1786 Boswell ventures to "promise that [his] Life of [his] revered Friend will be the richest piece of

3. On this notion, see Jean H. Hagstrum, *The Sister Arts*, pp. 11-12, 129, 247, and *passim*. On the grapes and curtain, see p. 24.

Biography that has ever appeared. The Bullion will be immense, whatever defects there may be in the workmanship" (*Corr—Life,* p. 146). Without denying the immensity of the bullion recent students of the *Life* have praised Boswell's workmanship. This has not always been easy, for Boswell's "arrangement" of materials has long occasioned criticism. The arguments are all by now familiar: the book is too heavily weighted to the final years of Johnson's life; coherent chronological arrangement with proper stress of each year and proper balancing of material does not exist; there is considerable filler, much of it dull, etc. However, Boswell's recent commentators (particularly Paul Alkon) have countered this criticism with some success, and Boswell's shaping, particularly the shaping of discrete scenes, has been praised extensively, despite Boswell's own claims and implicit theoretical orientation. My point will be, to return to Boswell's metaphor, that it is impossible to speak of the bullion without discussing the workmanship. The collector of materials collects with purposes and directions in mind. The purposes and directions determine the nature of the collection and the manner in which the materials will be displayed or presented. Tidy separations of data and principles (in science), of perceivers and objects (in epistemology), and of details and overall personality and character (in biography) are impossible.

CHAPTER II

The Scientific Analogy

You know I am a Metaphysician in my own way, allways reflecting allways endeavouring to get a more perfect knowledge of the human mind. Every little circumstance which occurs in my life is to me an Experiment in Philosophy. . . . (Corr—Grange, p. 196)

M ark Longaker comments that Boswell's "work came as a perfect expression of an age which fostered minuteness and exhaustiveness of detail, patience, and truth" (*English Biography in the Eighteenth Century*, p. 474). To speak of minuteness, detail, patience, and truth in the eighteenth century is to speak of "science," a vast nexus of accomplishments which the seventeenth and eighteenth centuries put to multiple uses. The threat posed by seventeenth-century skepticism was, in the main, either diverted or neutralized by the methodology and resultant achievements of the ostensibly orthodox seventeenth-century scientists. English religious ideologists—very often scientists themselves—had enlisted the support of science in their attacks on infidelity and heterodoxy. Finally, these activities proved to be more of a holding action than a decisive victory but for a time the holding action was extremely effective. "Science" inspired or fostered other activities as well. Attempts were made to mimic Newtonian feats in the social sciences and elsewhere, and the scientist was enthroned as the enlightenment hero, a creative, humane figure who replaced the old model of the conqueror, the destructive barbarian whose name should be expunged from history texts in favor of those whose activities have benefited rather than ravaged mankind. The scientist conquered problems rather than peoples and, as Johnson and others were to point out, redefined and extended our sense of the extent of human capability. Intellectual historians continually remind us of these matters, and with good reason, for the extent to which "science" permeates the thought of the period is difficult to exaggerate.

Boswell's interest in and knowledge of science falls far short of Johnson's, but his attempts to imitate the practices of the scientist—as he perceives those practices—is easily demonstrated. Throughout the *Life* Boswell's terminology and practice suggest an attempt to mimic scientific procedure. Bronson discusses this aspect of Boswell's work:

His imagination was as inexhaustibly fertile in suggesting human experiments as his ingenuity was indefatigable in devising the machinery for carrying them out. The *Journal of a Tour to the Hebrides with Samuel Johnson, LL.D.* is the undying record of his greatest single experiment; but many of the most telling scenes in the *Life*, like the dinner at Dilly's, are equally vivid reports of smaller experiments, and the Journals contain the clinical record of scores of minor ones. (*Johnson Agonistes and Other Essays*, p. 81)

Hugh Amory speaks of "Boswell's experimental attitude toward Johnson" ("Boswell in Search of the Intentional Fallacy," p. 36); Sven Eric Molin describes him as "the ideal social scientist. While he consciously organizes the experiment, he is also neutral to it once it gets under way . . . " ("Boswell's Account of the Johnson-Wilkes Meeting," p. 320). This use of scientific metaphor on the part of Boswell's commentators is quite appropriate, for Boswell discusses himself and his activities in similar terms. He is a social or conversational *catalyst*, a man delighted with "that intellectual chymistry, which can separate good qualities from evil in the same person" (*Life*, III, 65), a comment which appears at the beginning of one of Boswell's most important "experiments," the bringing together of Johnson and Wilkes.

The questions which I would pose concern the extent to which Boswell's quasi-scientific method contributes to or detracts from the total effect of the *Life*. Does his "scientific" posture provide leverage or indicate naiveté? Are contemporary scientific activities germane to the writing of biography and, if so, does Boswell understand those activities? The answers which have been given to questions such as these are sometimes contradictory. George Mallory claims that Boswell "had . . . the scientific spirit and applied it to the greatest of all subjects . . . human nature." Mallory writes of Boswell's "acute observation, . . . delicate experiments, [and] methodical accuracy . . . " (*Boswell the Biographer*, pp. 241-42, 283; cf. pp. 256-66). F. L. Lucas, on the other hand, compares Boswell to "one of those vivisectors Johnson abhorred," and terms him "a kind of grotesque anthropologist" (*The Search for Good Sense*, pp. 270, 271). Lucas' judgment is partly affected by his personal biographical leanings. His real preference is for the type of biography which he himself writes so well, the brief biography "which attempts to omit nothing that is really vital, and to include nothing that is not; which can leave a unified impression, but not lay a staggering load upon the memory" (*The Search for Good Sense*, p. xi). Lucas distrusts the inclusion of undigested facts. He stresses biographical selectivity and fears the gross presentation of facts which obscure rather than reveal the true subject of biography: personality. In Lucas' words, the encyclopedic biography which neglects essentials can "be as tedious and unpractical as a walking-tour of Siberia" (*The Search for Good Sense*, p. 271). Without levelling charges against Boswell at this point, it is fair to say that Lucas isolates important issues: how discriminating is Boswell's accumulation of factual material and, more important, is there a careful and systematic shaping of that material. To what extent is Boswell's use of his materials guided by principle?

The eighteenth-century scientist is well aware of the complex relation between the collection and use of data, but the subtlety of this relationship is not mirrored in Boswell's biographical practice. His interest is more in the process of collection than the attendant process of utilization. Clarence Tracy argues that

Johnson "knew when he had enough facts, [while] Boswell's thirst for them [seems] unquenchable." Thus, the *Life* "may seem . . . superficial in spite of its richness of material" ("Boswell: The Cautious Empiricist," pp. 232-33). Tracy and Lucas are both concerned with the relation between what Tracy terms "the quantity of reliable information" and "the finality of [Boswell's] interpretation" of that information ("Johnson and the Art of Anecdote," p. 87). Because Boswell's stress falls upon the process of gathering we must be particularly careful in evaluating the manner in which he shapes the material once the gathering process has been accomplished.

In treating Boswell's "kind of manic pursuit of the facts," Wimsatt argues that Boswell sets "a standard for the most scrupulous biographers of later ages" ("Images of Samuel Johnson," p. 362). Such biographers are now often termed "scientific," but the adjective is not wholly appropriate for Boswell, who might be expected to speak of "specimen biography" rather than "scientific biography." It is the individual instance, the representative bit of data, which concerns him rather than the systematic pattern. Of course, "representative data" suggests a larger pattern. The bits of Johnsonian behavior which Boswell includes must be symptomatic of something; they are not simply selected at random. The point at issue is the sophistication of Boswell's pattern—do his "specimens" suggest something interesting and important? As eighteenth-century satires of quacks and virtuosi suggest, the process of collection may involve a pattern which does not merit the adjective "scientific."

Boswell is constantly at pains to indicate those aspects of Johnson's life from which we are to generalize:

Such *specimens* of the easy and playful conversation of the great Dr. Samuel Johnson are, I think, to be prized. . . . (*Life*, II, 16)

Let this serve as a *specimen* of what accessions of literature he was perpetually infusing into his mind. . . . (*Life*, II, 263)

How well Johnson himself could have executed a translation of [Boethius], we may judge from the following *specimen*. . . . (*Life*, I, 139)

In the Gentleman's Magazine . . . he inserted an "Ode on Winter," which is, I think, an admirable *specimen* of his genius for lyrick poetry. (*Life*, I, 182)

. . . Johnson's Prologue, which, as it is not long, I shall here insert, as a *proof* that his poetical talents were in no degree impaired. (*Life*, III, 114)

Such *evidences* of his unceasing ardour, both for "divine and human lore," . . . must make us . . . honour his spirit. . . . (*Life*, II, 289)

As a *proof* of Dr. Johnson's extraordinary powers of composition, it appears. . . . (*Life*, III, 62n)

"I [Sir William Forbes] consider this . . . worth preserving, as it marks, in a certain degree, Dr. Johnson's character." . . . Sir William Forbes's observation is very just. The anecdote . . . *proves*, in the strongest manner, the reverence and awe with which Johnson was regarded. . . . (*Life*, III, 85)

. . . the following correspondence affords a *proof* not only of his benevolence and conscientious readiness to relieve a good man from errour, but . . . [also] shews his extraordinary command of clear and forcible expression. (*Life*, IV, 149; my italics throughout)

As every reader of the *Life* is aware, such examples could be multiplied easily. Boswell is adept at identifying interesting details; it is his use of them which is troubling. On the one hand the details often illustrate matters which are either well known or self-evident. In other words, they are but a step away from undigested material; Boswell is accumulating and displaying them, not subtly shaping them. In the quotations above, for example, Boswell marshals a series of specimens and proofs but the end result is merely our being told that Johnson was an able conversationalist, an avid reader, a good translator and poet, a lover of knowledge, an extraordinary writer, a benevolent, forceful, and articulate man who was revered by his friends. Boswell's scientific metaphors for his activities point to such aspects of the scientist's work as its rigor, its precision, and the assiduity necessary for the collection and presentation of data. Boswell overlooks the fact that the organization of that data is also important. One might, for example, take great pains to assemble a vast collection of rocks but no geologist would organize them under such categories as "red," "white," "gray," "shiny," and "dirty." The principles of discrimination and categorization must be subtle and interesting.

Another troubling aspect of Boswell's use of details is his propensity for interpreting them from his own point of view, a perspective which often does not (or may not) square with Johnson's. In the process Johnson's attitudes are often misrepresented and the shaping of details involves falsification of the biographical subject. A noteworthy example of this is the scene in which Johnson and Boswell arrive in Oxford by post-coach in 1784:

He bore the journey very well, and seemed to feel himself elevated as he approached Oxford, that magnificent and venerable seat of Learning, Orthodoxy, and Toryism. (*Life*, IV, 284–85)

Johnson's "elevation" could be interpreted in numerous ways. It could indicate his abilities as a good traveler, his buoyant and youthful demeanor, his anticipation of meeting old friends, his response to landscape that is inherently beautiful or meaningful because of associations, perhaps even relief that the trip was over. Instead, we are presented with Orthodox, Tory, i.e. Boswellian, Oxford. Boswell's judgment here may be correct; he may be isolating the essential elements in Johnson's response, i.e., he may be reading Johnson's mind correctly. In order to do that, however, Boswell should provide us with the assurance that he does indeed understand Johnson's religion and politics— his sense of Orthodoxy and Toryism—and has an awareness of the essential facts of Johnson's association with Oxford (for example, how long Johnson was there as a student). Here, of course, Boswell is weak and it is not unreasonable to consider it a likely possibility that in the scene in question Boswell has transferred his own feelings to Johnson.

The falsification of detail on Boswell's part is not always demonstrable. The superficial use of detail, however, is om-nipresent. More often than not, Boswell's instances, specimens, or "proofs" merely demonstrate that Johnson is kind, quick-witted, or articulate, that he has a good memory or is able to compose rapidly. There is nothing false here but nothing particularly engaging either:

In 1783, he was more severely afflicted than ever, as will appear in the course of his correspondence; but still the same ardour for literature, the same constant piety, the same kindness for his friends, and the same vivacity, both in conversation and writing, distinguished him. (*Life*, IV, 163)

The problem partially results from the fact that Boswell's image of Johnson is itself far too general; thus the details which are employed to illustrate that image are used in superficial fashion. The final words of the *Life* point up Boswell's ultimate sense of Johnson: a man to be regarded "with admiration and reverence," in short, a man of both mighty accomplishments and essential personal goodness. The estimate is wholly accurate, of course, but its uses are limited in the extreme:

I give this account fairly, as a specimen of that unhappy temper with which this *great and good man* had occasionally to struggle. . . . (*Life*, III, 345)

We surely cannot but admire the benevolent exertions of this *great and good man*. . . . (*Life*, III, 368)

So truly humble were the thoughts which this *great and good man* entertained. . . . (*Life*, IV, 410)

. . . my [Warren Hastings'] veneration for your *great and good* friend, Dr. Johnson. . . . (*Life*, IV, 66)

. . . I will venture to predict, that this specimen of the colloquial talents and extemporaneous effusions of my illustrious fellow-traveller will become still more valuable, when . . . no other memorial of this *great and good man* shall remain, but the following Journal. . . . (*Tour*, V, 4)

I believe I told your Lordship [Lord Kames] before I left England that I had obtained the friendship of Mr. Samuel Johnson. I look upon this as the happiest incident in my life. The conversation of that *great and good man* has formed me to manly virtue. . . . (*Boswell on the Grand Tour, 1764*, p. 111; my italics throughout)

Criticism of Boswell in this regard involves a question of judgment. There is certainly no *a priori* weakness in a biography whose image of the biographical subject is a general one. Ideally the biographical subject should exemplify important aspects of common human experience. The question is one of degree. In the case of Johnson, in my judgment, "great and good" is excessively general. As a *terminus ad quem* it leaves us with the sense that Boswell's selection of details could be as haphazard and undiscerning as he pleased, for the ultimate conclusion of the details—that image which should also determine their initial selection—is the barest commonplace. In his Essay on Epitaphs Johnson writes that "the praise [in epitaphs] ought not to be general, because the mind is lost in the extent of any indefinite idea, and cannot be affected with what it cannot comprehend. When we hear only of a good or great man, we know not in what class to place him, nor have any notion of his character, distinct from that of a thousand others . . . " (1825 *Works*, V, 264). Boswell, however, is not troubled by this in the least. His own treatment of the question of the importance of "image" is strikingly cavalier.

As he approaches the conclusion of the *Life*, Boswell is put off by the need to write Johnson's "character." Reluctantly he does it, but he notes that "the greatest part of the sketch" is adopted from the *Journal of a Tour to the Hebrides* (IV, 425n). His attitude toward his readers is here particularly jarring:

I shall endeavour to acquit myself of that part of my biographical undertaking, however difficult it may be to do that which many of my readers will do better for themselves. (IV, 425)

In short, the "character" is largely superfluous, for the reader—armed with Boswell's specimens, proofs, and details—can form the "character" by himself. Ideally, the "character" should arise from the totality of available material; it is the responsibility of the biographer and not of the reader to examine that material. Moreover, Boswell's sense of the volume of material which he is presenting is very misleading. We are given much less than we think, part of Boswell's genius lying in his ability to mask this fact. The material presented is considerable compared to that offered by Boswell's biographical predecessors, but it is, inescapably, a small fragment of Johnson's experience. The number of letters, for example, is impressive in contrast to that offered by a biographer like Walton, but only about one-fifth of Johnson's letters are included. Boswell also prides himself on his scenes and conversations but the "scenes" which cover four to five pages may treat four to five hours (or more) of experience. Assuming a very conservative rate of fifty words per minute of conversation we would have a transcript of sixty-odd pages in typescript for a five-hour discussion. The scenes and conversations are epitomes, précis, specimens. Boswell's "Flemish picture" might "mark the most minute particulars" but it could only mark an infinitesimal portion of them. Boswell's posture, however, conceals the selectivity of his method at the same time as it downplays the importance of an "image" to guide that process of selection. If, for example, we are only to receive a paragraph or two as a substitute for a full account of an evening's experience, it is crucial that the most important, most representative, and most instructive material be presented. The basis for selection—the overall sense of the biographical subject—is crucial.

Boswell's minimal stress of systematic shaping did not escape his contemporaries' criticism. His reviewer in the *Oracle* (23 June 1791) commented as follows:

We think, upon a deliberate perusal of much of these volumes, that the character of JOHNSON stands nearly as it previously stood . . . that his Biographer's zeal has been blind and undistinguishing, and that the *Gold Dust* should have been *ingotted* before it was presented to the Public.[1]

In a famous judgment, Lockhart writes: "Never did any man tell a story with such liveliness and fidelity, and yet contrive to leave so strong an impression that he did not himself understand it,"[2] a source—for Lockhart—of the *Life's* charm, though the comment underscores the disparity between Boswell's raw materials and his comprehension and use of them.

1. Cited by Lucyle Werkmeister, *Jemmie Boswell and the London Daily Press, 1785-1795*, p. 31.
2. Cited by Francis R. Hart, "Boswell and the Romantics," p. 49.

As Boswell's contemporaries and nineteenth-century successors realized, the use of conversations and private correspondence (one of Boswell's major achievements) is touchy indeed and the assumption of authentic revelation of personality, based on the nature of these materials, is highly suspect. Such materials must be used with the greatest discretion, discretion based on an overarching, sophisticated sense of the biographical subject.[3]

Paul Alkon reminds us of the fact that Boswell did not use all of the material at his disposal; it will not do to accuse him of simpleminded inclusion of everything he touched ("Boswellian Time," p. 253).[4] Nevertheless, the relationship which Boswell posits between the collection of his material and the shaping of it is quite clear. The former procedure is the more important one and the two procedures are separable. In Boswell's judgment, his method involves a degree of rigor and authenticity analogous to that found in the practice of contemporary scientists. It is useful to pursue this analogy in more detail.

Goethe comments:

Man is born not to solve the problems of the universe, but to find out where the problem begins, and then to restrain himself within the limits of the comprehensible. His faculties are not sufficient to measure the actions of the universe; and an attempt to explain the outer world by reason is, with his narrow point of view, but a vain endeavor. (Eckermann, *Words of Goethe*, p. 130)

The judgment may seem curious amid the enthusiasm of a post-Newtonian world, but much of that enthusiasm was generated by "Newtonians" who failed to understand the precise nature of their master's accomplishment. Goethe's view accurately mirrors the ideology of seventeenth- and eighteenth-century English scientists, who were more interested in restraint than "explanation." One of the best and most famous statements of

---

3. On this, see Hart, "Boswell and the Romantics," pp. 52-54.

4. One cannot help but point out the fact that important, troubling material was carefully *excluded* from the *Life*. This is, in many ways, a more serious failing. Trivia and minutiae may try a reader's patience; suppression and bowdlerizing falsify the biographical subject.

their methodological posture is to be found at the conclusion of Newton's *Opticks:*

As in Mathematicks, so in Natural Philosophy, the Investigation of difficult Things by the Method of Analysis, ought ever to precede the Method of Composition. This Analysis consists in making Experiments and Observations, and in drawing general Conclusions from them by Induction, and admitting of no Objections against the Conclusions, but such as are taken from Experiments, or other certain Truths. For Hypotheses are not to be regarded in experimental Philosophy. And although the arguing from Experiments and Observations by Induction be no Demonstration of general Conclusions; yet it is the best way of arguing which the Nature of Things admits of, and may be looked upon as so much the stronger, by how much the Induction is more general. And if no Exception occur from Phaenomena, the Conclusion may be pronounced generally. But if at any time afterwards any Exception shall occur from Experiments, it may then begin to be pronounced with such Exceptions as occur. (p. 404)

This particular formulation is complicated by the fact that Newton is here comparing the procedures of mathematics with those of empirical science; in practice the two are very often joined. Essentially Newton presents Royal Society methodology, what Popkin and others usually term "constructive skepticism," the movement from data to principles (cast in mathematical terms if possible) followed by the testing of those principles by further observation and experiment, a method designed to yield a descriptive rather than an explanatory account of nature, an account which is always open to revision in light of new data, an account valued in proportion to its usefulness. No explanations of ultimate causes are claimed; the method steers a course between uncritical dogmatism and radical skepticism.[5]

Newton, however, presents particular methodological problems, for his pronouncements are scattered and seemingly inconsistent. As Professor Randall argues in his celebrated study of Newton's methodology, Newton sought a system of ex-

5. Among the many studies of these issues, one of the most important and most useful is Van Leeuwen's *The Problem of Certainty in English Thought, 1630-1690.*

perimentally verifiable mathematical laws, but a system which did not pretend to reveal the ultimate *cause* of those laws, for such an explanation—in the eyes of the Royal Society—is beyond human capability. However, while Newton admits that he has found only the law and not the cause of gravitation, he believes that he does know the cause of the laws of motion: the force of inertia.[6] A second methodological split bears on the first. His practice and theory collide over the issue of his "absolutes" and his use of mathematics, his mathematics pushing him beyond the realm of that which may be experienced. Here is Randall:

Newton's real world is therefore made up of absolute masses endowed with an absolute force of inertia, and perhaps with a force of "gravitation," in absolute motion in absolute space and time; while sense experience supplies no evidence for any of these concepts.

Newton's procedure implied that the concern of science was with mathematical relations in the experienced world. Yet his empirical logic drove him to assume that the terms of those relations are not in the experienced world at all, and yet are the only reality. The absolute masses of classical mechanics, instead of being taken as mathematical abstractions or isolates, were regarded as the sole components of Nature. Here is a cardinal illustration of what Whitehead has called the "fallacy of misplaced concreteness." (pp. 350, 353-54)

The problem is exacerbated by the fact that many of Newton's marmoreal statements are mathematical ones. L. L. Laudan comments that the *"Principia* seemed to have established, almost overnight, new standards for rigour of thought, clarity of intuition, economy of expression and, *above all*, the certainty of its conclusions" ("Thomas Reid and the Newtonian Turn of British Methodological Thought," p. 103). It is here that we must resist the enthusiasm of many of Newton's followers and be reminded of Voltaire's definition of Newtonian fluxions, "the art of exactly numbering and measuring that of which we cannot even conceive the existence" (*Philosophical Letters*, p. 79) and Einstein's judgment that "as far as the propositions of

6. John Herman Randall, Jr., "Newton's Natural Philosophy: Its Problems and Consequences," pp. 340-44 and *passim.*

mathematics refer to reality they are not certain, and in so far as they are certain they do not refer to reality."[7]

Within the context of contemporary science, Boswell's procedure will not do. His stress of collection at the expense of systematic organization and shaping would associate him with the benighted empirics attacked by Bacon, the blind, indiscriminate gatherers. On the other hand, his attempts at compelling authenticity and accuracy mimic the search for mathematical certainty which represents a heterodox facet of Newton's method. The more conservative Royal Society—and, to an important extent, Newtonian—approach offers *descriptions* which are far distant from the rigors of mathematics, accounts aptly described by Plato's Timaeus:

> You must be satisfied if our account is as likely as any, remembering that both I and you who are sitting in judgment on it are merely human, and should not look for anything more than a likely story in such matters. (*Timaeus and Critias*, p. 41)

The "likely story" is all that the Royal Society would promise— scientific "explanations" which were, at best, analogies of actual processes. D'Alembert summarizes the matter precisely:

> Doomed as we are to be ignorant of the essence and inner contexture of bodies, the only resource remaining for our sagacity is to try at least to grasp the analogy of phenomena, and to reduce them all to a small number of primitive and fundamental facts.[8]

Hume writes that "all our reasonings concerning matter of fact are founded on a species of *analogy*" (*An Inquiry Concerning Human Understanding*, p. 112); Kant comments that we study things "according to the analogies of experience which determine in general all real combinations in experience."[9] Moreover, as Hoyt Trowbridge has ably demonstrated ("Scattered Atoms of

---

7. Cited by I. Bernard Cohen, *Franklin and Newton*, pp. 3-4.

8. Cited by Henry Guerlac, "Where the Statue Stood: Divergent Loyalties to Newton in the Eighteenth Century," p. 330.

9. *Critique of Pure Reason*, pp. 174-75. On the eighteenth century and the notion of analogy see Eric Rothstein, *Systems of Order and Inquiry in Later Eighteenth-Century Fiction*, pp. 11-17 and *passim*.

Probability"), Locke's probabilistic epistemology depends upon the notion of comparison and analogy; in this regard pertinent applications to, for example, Johnson's literary criticism are demonstrable. In short, the scientist seeks "explanations" that are really analogies for natural processes, just as the biographer seeks to create a simulacrum for a human life. That life cannot be presented directly and completely because of media differences and time/space limitations. Thus the biographer presents—through print usually, but not exclusively—a pattern or structure which will serve as a substitute which aids understanding. Boswell's "scientific analogy," his biographical method which suggests scientific procedures, mimics bad science. This may be directly traceable to the fact that Boswell simply lacks sophistication (and interest) in scientific matters. He is equally shaky with philosophy. He could, for example, have seen Berkeley's continuing criticism of Newton's "absolutes" and of "Newtonian certainty," a criticism which is both conservative and forward-looking. Basically, Berkeley espouses the methodology of the Royal Society, but in his attacks on materialism, "abstraction," and mathematization and in his stress of valuation, vision, spirit, and individual perception he earns the praise of nearly every Romantic poet. His work, in fact, is a useful gloss on Boswell's, particularly something like the London Journal, but Boswell—largely with his age— is unable to come to terms with Berkeley's thought. He is equally inept with Hume, whose works always seem to upset but never to instruct him. Hume, for example, argues in the celebrated essay on taste that geometrical exactitude is not germane to poetry. Poetry's rules may be based on experience but absolute rigor cannot be demanded of either poetry or the criticism of poetry (Of the Standard of Taste and Other Essays, p. 7 esp.). Unlike Boswell, Hume is very wary of terms like "authentic" and "perfect." "Certainty," of course, he denies definitively.

The orthodox scientific model is analogous to the ideal biographical model. The scientist confronts a relationship of successive alternations. Data are taken; principles are shaped, and so on. "Essential" explanations are impossible; all that is offered are analogies, likely stories. The biographer's task is to produce a book whose relation to the life of its subject can only be analogical as well. The biographer can neither offer a final, essential account of his subject, nor can he marshal *all* of the data of the subject's life. His "image" of his subject, like the "explanation" offered by the scientist is at best *useful* (an old Baconian principle, of course, and one which Berkeley seizes upon in his criticism of Newton). The biographer's "image" affects his selection and use of his material but it should correspond with or epitomize the multiple dimensions of the subject which are accessible through the totality of the material. Material is examined; an "image" forms; the "image" is tested by the examination of further material; the "image" is altered, clarified, redefined; the book is shaped on the basis of the "image" which hopefully will help to explain or clarify new aspects of the subject which later arise. There is no separation of material and "image" and there is no pretense concerning completeness, certitude, or absolute authenticity. The process is a dynamic one, but, simultaneously, a systematic one.

Boswell's posture, it seems to me, is naive both with regard to biographical and scientific practices. Johnson's awareness of the importance of systematic shaping is here closer to the mark. As Allan Cunningham commented, "The chief fault of [Boswell's] performance is, that it wants the splendid summary, and final judgment of character, which forms the crowning glory to the *Lives of the Poets*." With Boswell, "we are left to draw our own conclusions . . . and the consequence is, that every one forms a mental character according to his abilities or prejudices, and nothing is fixed or defined . . ." (Clifford, *Biography as an Art*, p. 88). Part of that character which each reader forms will also be affected by Boswell's curious omissions and sometimes even more curious inclusions. He will also be affected by Boswell's own abilities and prejudices. In fairness to Boswell, the obvious must be stated: Johnson's impatience with the laborious process of gathering and examining material results in far less ambitious biographies than the *Life* and the "images" which emerge in Johnsonian life-writing are more the result of insight than any examination of the material in its totality. On the other hand, Johnson wrote dozens of lives, Boswell only two—his own and Johnson's. In a sense, Johnson was correct when he complained of Boswell's having only two subjects. The problem, however, lies not in the paucity of subjects but in the confusion of them. Despite the pressure of textbooks, college course descriptions, and popular lore, Johnson and Boswell *can* be separated. Unfortunately, the difficulty of effecting that separation was as great for Boswell as it is for us, a matter to which we will soon return.

CHAPTER III

Artifice and Reality

It is amazing how much every thing depends on the state of our minds at the time, and how little the state of any one's mind is known to others. (PP, XVI, 11)

Boswell's 1783 Journal entry is the sort of truism which one encounters frequently in a period whose epistemology underscores (among other things) the subjective nature of perception. Hume's treatment of causality had, in a sense, compounded the problems raised by Berkeley's denial of the primary/secondary qualities distinction. Berkeley had shown that claims concerning "primary" qualities rested on a process of "abstraction" of which the mind is not capable. In the process Berkeley challenged the attention which had previously been accorded the so-called material substratum underlying objects which are perceived by us in terms of secondary qualities. In turning his attention from the question of substance to that of causation, Hume recognized Berkeley's insights and added new ones, particularly the denial of any ultimate certitude concerning causal relationships and the attendant necessity to base our decisions, judgments, and predictions on what may loosely be termed *feelings.*

Despite the label of "skeptic" so frequently affixed to him,

Hume writes in opposition to pyrrhonist and other extreme varieties of skepticism.[1] He points up the schizophrenic nature of the extreme skeptic's lot: his principles should drive him to a state of utter inactivity but the demands of nature force him to act and to choose. Moreover, the extreme skeptic overlooks the fact that his principles rest on sand. Because belief is the result of *feelings* it is not subject to rational dispute and challenge. Hume's posture is not unlike that of the Restoration and eighteenth-century scientist, who also denied the possibility of ultimate, causal explanations but who simultaneously attempted to enhance our understanding of nature. Hume's focus is human nature and very often, particularly in the *Treatise*, his comments echo the ideological pronouncements of the scientists.[2] The interconnections of science and philosophy in the period are demonstrable. In the previous chapter I attempted to treat the overarching pattern of the *Life*, the relation between details and final "image," through an analogy to scientific methodology. Here I wish to discuss the "scenes" in the *Life*, those individual units which have received so much attention, in the context of epistemology. It should be noted, however, that science might work just as well, for as I have just indicated, science and philosophy did not operate *in vacuo* in the period but rather in relation to one another. The "epistemological analogy" is not unlike the scientific one.

The scientific analogy suggests a relation between scientist and subject which admits of no simple division or dividing line, but is rather one of interchange and interconnection. The epistemological relation between perceiver and object is of a similar nature. Hume, for example, treats the manner in which an object or experience is assimilated and evaluated in the

---

1. See Richard H. Popkin, "David Hume: His Pyrrhonism and His Critique of Pyrrhonism."

2. See, for example, *Treatise*, p. 43: "Here then is the only expedient, from which we can hope for success in our philosophical researches, to leave the tedious lingering method . . . and . . . march up directly to the capital or center of these sciences, to human nature itself. . . . And as the science of man is the only solid foundation for the other sciences, so the only solid foundation we can give to this science itself must be laid on experience and observation."

context of past experience, the fact that an elaborate body of associations is brought to bear on each experience and enables us to deal with it. Fortunately, there is considerable overlap among our experiences. We assimilate and evaluate in similar fashion based on common experience. Thus we are not locked into a state of absolute subjectivism. Our parallel responses to common experience generates interest (especially with Hume and Johnson) in the principle of consensus and in the relation between the particular and the general. "Unique" experiences are often common; very "personal" emotions are very common ones. We are, in a sense, most fully "human" when we are truly ourselves. Jung comments on this process:

Can experience with the objective world save us from subjective prejudgments? Is not every experience, even in the best of circumstances, to a large extent subjective interpretation? On the other hand, the subject also is an objective fact, a piece of the world. What issues from it comes, after all, from the universal soil, just as the rarest and strangest organism is none the less supported and nourished by the earth which we all share in common. It is precisely the most subjective ideas which, being closest to nature and to the living being, deserve to be called the truest. (*Modern Man in Search of a Soul,* pp. 115-16)

It is the responsibility of the life-writer to demonstrate the relationship between the particular and the general, to show the manner in which each life recapitulates a larger pattern. As the period realized, utter "uniqueness" is utterly dull and irrelevant. Significance (as E. D. Hirsch argues) is based on relationships, not on units in isolation.

A crucial relationship for the life-writer, indeed for every literary artist, is that between what is crudely termed "reality" and "artifice": the "external," "objective" subject and the artist's shaping of it. Indeed, the separation or confusion of artifice and reality have been among the most common thematic mainstays. What concerns me is the manner in which the eighteenth-century artist uses the artifice/reality dichotomy for both thematic and rhetorical leverage. The manipulation of that dichotomy is the basis for some of the most effective passages in the period's literature, particularly its prose literature. A common pattern involves the establishment of a line separating reality from the shaping of reality. The life/art distinction is then systematically blurred as the artist traverses the line with both subtlety and rapidity. The basis for the procedure is partially to be found in the period's epistemological insights. I will argue that the procedure informs certain sections of Boswell's work, while a confused version of the procedure flaws others. The procedure demands rigorous control, control that is usually maintained when Boswell writes of himself but often lost when he writes of Johnson.

Art and life, the artificial and the "real," cannot be neatly separated. Their mutual relationship is a sophisticated one. Bachelard comments that "it is impossible to receive the psychic benefit of poetry unless . . . two functions of the human psyche—the function of the real and the function of the unreal—are made to cooperate" (*The Poetics of Space*, p. xxxi). Goethe praises the actor Lecain as "one of the few who know how to turn the artificial completely into nature, and nature completely into the artificial" (*Autobiography*, II, 107). Later in *Dichtung und Wahrheit* Goethe records the comment of Merck:

"Thy striving," said he, "thy unswerving effort is, to give a poetic form to the real: others seek to give reality to the so-called poetic, to the imaginative; and of that nothing will ever come but stupid stuff." Whoever apprehends the immense difference between these two modes of action, whoever insists and acts upon this conviction, has reached the solution of a thousand other things. (II, 367)

Cassirer notes that in entitling his autobiography *Poetry and Truth* Goethe "did not mean that he had inserted into the narrative of his life any imaginary or fictitious elements. He wanted to discover and describe the truth about his life; but this truth could only be found by giving to the isolated and dispersed facts of his life a poetical, that is a symbolic, shape" (*An Essay on Man*, p. 57). Cassirer's comment implies a unilateral relationship—the "real" is shaped—but as Cassirer is well aware, the process can become far more complex. One may shape the "real" but also reify the artificial. The dates and facts of an individual life may be treated almost novelistically but the dreams and fantasies of the individual consciousness can be treated as compelling "realities." Wilde points out in "The Decay of Lying" that despite the apparent redundancy, art truly reifies the "real." Life imitates art; life is the mirror, art the reality:

Nature is no great mother who has borne us. She is our creation. It is in our brain that she quickens to life. Things are because we see them, and what we see, and how we see it, depends on the arts that have influenced us. (p. 683)

Comments such as this are extremely useful for the student of Boswell. Wimsatt has termed Boswell "a visionary of the real"; "he [has] a way of responding to mere facts so as to invest them with a kind of hyperactuality and heightened import" ("Images of Samuel Johnson," p. 359). To return to Wilde's comment, Boswell sees in very special ways and has been influenced in very special ways. From time to time his life directly imitates art and for much of the time "reality" for Boswell corresponds with the manner in which he has shaped and fashioned it. When there is conflict between life and Boswell's desire to shape it, his responses can be curious ones. In *Hypochondriack* 66 he makes a comment that had been anticipated seven years earlier in his Journal: "Sometimes it has occurred to me that a man should not live more than he can record, as a farmer should not have a larger crop than he can gather in."[3] The manipulation of the art/life relationship results in some of Boswell's most effective set pieces; it also, however, can result in set pieces which falsify his biographical subject.

Boswell can use the art/life relationship in simple unilateral fashion: art is employed to "heighten" or "intensify" life. At his best, however, Boswell is able to achieve effects which parallel the complex accomplishments of his great contemporaries. It may be argued that literary manipulation of the art/life division mirrors the kind of interaction previously discussed in the context of scientific method. In science, data lead to principles;

3. *Hypochondriack*, II, 259. Cf. Paul Alkon, "Boswellian Time," p. 241: "In this remark Boswell puts the usual relationship backwards . . . instead of advocating adjustment of literary time to real time, he toys with the opposite adjustment of real time to possible literary time. . . ."

principles are altered based on new data, etc. The data and principles—the particular and the general—are locked in an interdependent, dynamic relationship. In epistemology a parallel pattern exists. As Kant would argue, the perceiver apprehends "nature" in terms of categories. "Nature" cannot be examined as something knowable in and of itself, apart from human perception. In Humean terms, "nature" is perceived in terms of our prior experience of it. Our relationship to the object of our perceptions involves human needs, limitations, and valuation—a point particularly stressed by Berkeley. Again, the relationship is an interconnected one, one that cannot be divided into discrete units. To talk of objects is to talk of perceivers; to talk of principles is to talk of data.

The literary pattern is analogous to these patterns. Beginning with the initial division of art and life or artifice and reality, we suddenly find ourselves amidst an interconnected pattern. Life may, in Wilde's term, mirror art, but that art mirrors life which mirrors art, and so on. In a play one may, for example, encounter real, that is historical, people satirized under tag names. The names suggest caricature, and thus artifice, but the artifice mirrors life, for these people—the objects of the satire—act like caricatures in "real" life. In a slightly different but still relevant sense of the term, their "real" lives are artificial, and hence "realistically" portrayed in the theatre. In a context such as this the artist demonstrates his abilities by multiplying the relationships (traversing the art/life line ever more rapidly) without disturbing the basic pattern of highly controlled reverberations.

In *Spectator* 414, Addison—a figure of immense importance for Boswell—treats the by then well-worn subject of the antithesis of nature and art. He observes "that there is generally in Nature something more Grand and August, than what we meet with in the Curiosities of Art," but he is not content to opt for one over the other. His commentary on their relationship focuses on interconnectedness:

But tho' there are several of these wild Scenes, that are more delightful than any artificial Shows; yet we find the Works of Nature still more pleasant, the more they resemble those of Art. . . .

If the Products of Nature rise in Value, according as they more or less resemble those of Art, we may be sure that artificial Works receive a greater Advantage from their Resemblance of such as are natural. . . .

It is the interrelation, not the separation or competition, of nature and art which should command our attention, and as I argued earlier, the utilization of that relationship results in some of the most effective set pieces and passages in eighteenth-century literature. The art/life pattern is especially useful in that body of material which Watt, among others, terms the "literature of experience," that literature which treats historical realities through the use of complex literary devices, a literature which includes Boswell's *Life* as one of its most distinguished examples. The pattern also appears in fiction and, of course, in painting.

One of the works which profoundly affected Boswell is the *Beggar's Opera*. Hogarth's final version of the *Beggar's Opera*, III, ii (originally done for Rich) signals, in Paulson's judgment, Hogarth's attainment of maturity as a painter (*Hogarth: His Life, Art, and Times*, I, 188). The basic design is highly stylized. Hogarth uses the judgment of Hercules pattern and positions Macheath between Lucy and Polly, who entreat their fathers on his behalf. However, as Paulson notes, Hogarth makes it clear that the personages "are not highwaymen, lovers, jailers, and fences, but actors on a stage . . . the stage curtains are in plain sight, as are members of the audience seated on both sides and [in several earlier versions] behind the actors" (p. 185). In one preliminary version Hogarth had painted a stone prison floor; in the final version he returns to wooden boards, thus underscoring the artifice of the stage. In the first version the audience appears as a series of caricatures; in the final version these figures are rendered realistically. Rich, his friends, and Gay appear in the picture. In the audience Hogarth places the Duke of Bolton, positioned so that his eye meets Polly's (Lavinia Fenton's). Polly's right arm, pointed toward Macheath in earlier versions, is now pointed toward Bolton so as to indicate their relationship in "real" life. Paulson comments that "the actors [are] juxtaposed on the stage with their roles and with aristocratic members of the audience [so that] thematic and psychological tensions [can] be suggested" (p. 185). Hogarth's art represents something real, a scene in a playhouse with actors and an identifiable audience, but the painting is artificial in its stylized structure and its subject is a scene in a play—an artifice—whose subject is (among other things) the values and activities of a type of real, public figure which are so twisted as to justify excessively stylized (i.e. operatic) representation and the most transparent type of tag name, an artifice mirroring the "artificial" real, presented before a real audience whose participation in artificiality is represented through subtle links with the personages on stage. The painting is simultaneously static, controlled, and vibrant.

In eighteenth-century fiction, similar effects are frequently sought. *Tristram Shandy* is probably the best case in point: a work whose thematic interest and rhetorical techniques are demonstrably influenced by insights in epistemology, and a book with which Boswell was much taken. The manipulation of the artifice/reality relationship is common throughout the book. Numerous scenes could be used to illustrate the pattern. A particularly effective one is the dinner at Didius'. The scene satirizes "real" individuals, some of whom have been identified. They are given obvious tag names, suggesting, in most cases, their characteristic trait or activity. These real people with fictional names embodying real meanings are brought together through the artificial form of the banquet scene, common in classical satire (the tag names are "classical") but just as common in York (or any other) society. Real people and real issues (popes, jurists, papal pronouncements, legal commentaries, etc.) are juxtaposed with preposterous action, especially the journey of the hot chestnut into the hiatus in Phutatorius' breeches. This action enables Sterne to test very real theories of pain and pleasure, an issue discussed by such figures as Locke, Hartley, and Burke. In a magnificent manipulation of the art/life dichotomy, a nostrum is prescribed for Phutatorius' burn which involves an outrageous collapsing of the art/life division so that art is applied directly to life:

——Can you tell me, quoth *Phutatorius,* speaking to *Gastripheres* who sat next to him,——for one would not apply to a surgeon in so foolish an affair,——can you tell me, *Gastripheres,* what is best to take out the fire?——Ask *Eugenius,* said *Gastripheres*——That greatly depends, said *Eugenius,* pretending ignorance of the adventure, upon the nature of the part——If it is a tender part, and a part which can conveniently be wrapt up——It is both the one and the other, replied *Phutatorius,* laying his hand as he spoke, with an emphatical nod of his head, upon the part in question, and lifting up his right leg at the same time to ease and ventilate it—If that is the case, said *Eugenius,* I would advise you, *Phutatorius,* not to tamper with it by any means; but if you will send to the next printer, and trust your cure to such a simple thing as a soft sheet of paper just come off the press——you need do nothing more than twist it round—The damp paper, quoth *Yorick* (who sat next to his friend *Eugenius*) though I know it has a refreshing coolness in it—— yet I presume is no more than the vehicle——and that the oil and lamp-black with which the paper is so strongly impregnated, does the business——(pp. 324-25)

Presumably we are to speculate naughtily on the contents of the set-off, perhaps also, considering the meaning of Phutatorius' name, on its possible audience. This all coexists neatly with Sterne's quite serious examination of his central theme of isolation and skewed communication which is introduced by Phutatorius' initially misunderstood "Zounds!" "The true cause of his examination," Tristram indecently notes, "lay at least a yard below" (p. 319).

One of the crucial elements in a passage such as this or in a painting such as Hogarth's is control. When art/life distinctions and relations are manipulated, the most serious danger is that of confusion. If art and life are unconsciously transposed, if one is mistaken for the other, the pattern is shattered, though that in itself can constitute an effective subject, as in Partridge's reaction to Garrick's *Hamlet* in *Tom Jones,* XVI, v.

The playhouse is, for various reasons, an appropriate and useful arena for utilizing these techniques and treating these kinds of themes. Boswell was nearly addicted to the theatre, as all are aware, and uses stage terminology in describing the *Life.* He tells Erskine he is going "to write Dr. Johnson's life in Scenes" (*PP,* XIV, 132) and in a famous passage tells Bishop Percy that his "is the best plan of Biography that can be conceived; for [his] Readers will as near as may be accompany Johnson in his progress, and as it were see each scene as it happened" (*Corr—Life*, p. 265). These scenes, particularly the meeting with Wilkes, have received considerable attention and have resulted in a good deal of praise for Boswell's abilities. I wish to discuss them in light of my foregoing discussion.

Geoffrey Scott writes that "the Johnson record, in the Journal, had fallen quite automatically into a series of *tableaux*, like the rest of Boswell's social life" (*PP*, VI, 161). One of the most successful accounts of Boswell's social life is that portion of the Journal covering the 1762-1763 sojourn in London. The London Journal, as it is usually termed, is the most accomplished section of Boswell's personal record. Its popular success has probably been due in large part to its accounts of Boswell's womanizing, but Boswell's real interest and concern in that portion of the Journal centers around roles and role playing far more than orgiastic indulgence. He has been praised for his rendition of his activities, and in terms which echo the life/art pattern treated above. Here is Frederick Kiley:

By selection, omission, and perhaps improvisation, the conscious artistry of Boswell, the writer, translates Boswell, the adventurer, into a third Boswell, the literary figure, a hero of a work that organizes life to fit the formal demands of fiction. By shifting the conventional illusion of fiction—that the literary happenings in the story are a form of reality—Boswell, in the *London Journal*, posits that real life follows a literary design. ("Boswell's Literary Art in the *London Journal*," p. 632)

With regard to the Louisa episode, Paul Fussell comments on "the pleasure [Boswell] derives from playing the role of an actor, an actor who in turn enjoys playing the part of a fine seducer" ("The Force of Literary Memory in Boswell's *London Journal*," p. 355), a seducer, I would add, intriguing with "an actress who had played many a fine lady's part" (p. 149). In seducing Louisa he seduces all of the characters she has played and thus, to an extent, transforms himself into her respective dramatic counterparts. He assumes another role, that of Restoration wit, and displays his qualifications for the part by indulging in vulgar puns: "I patrolled up and down Fleet Street, thinking on London, the seat of Parliament and the seat of pleasure, and seeming to myself as one of the wits in King Charles the Second's time" (p. 140). After he is infected by Louisa his role shifts to that of a "man of honour." He seeths with just outrage, plays his part with acumen, and renders it in dialogue with editorial comments and stage directions. The clap may bring Boswell momentarily to earth after the night of bliss and days of artifice, but it provides him the opportunity to observe himself in another role; he can contemplate his clapped self. In his sexual activities there is even a touch of role playing in his use of "armour" though the metaphor is moribund.

Boswell's imaginative world is the world of real importance to him. He may have difficulty comprehending subjectivism but he has no difficulty indulging in it. The Journal begins in precisely this spirit:

The scene of being a son setting out from home for the wide world and the idea of being my own master, pleased me much. . . . As I passed the Cross, the cadies and the chairmen bowed and seemed to say, "God prosper long our noble Boswell." (p. 41)

He is not involved in an identity search. In a sense he "knows" himself but continues to seek external proof or verification of his beliefs concerning his character, appearance, and personality. To return to the phrasing of my second chapter, he seeks *specimens:*

Upon my soul, not a bad specimen of a man. However my particular notions may alter, I always preserve these great and worthy qualities. (p. 80)

But I cannot help thinking [such a little incident] amusing, and valuing it as a specimen of my own tenderness of disposition and willingness to relieve my fellow-creatures. (p. 100)

Even when his actions are affected he thinks he knows what or who he should be, yet he continues to enjoy various roles. He is "a true-born Old Englishman" (p. 86), Sir Richard Steele "sitting in judgment on a new comedy" (p. 177), Mr. Spectator (p. 244), Captain Macheath (p. 264) and perhaps even Samuel Johnson:

No place can be more favourable for meditation than such a retirement as this [Johnson's] garret. I could not help indulging a scheme of taking it for myself many years hence. . . . (p. 311)

He reduces himself to literary form through the use of dialogue (even dialogue with his guardian angel—p. 77) and through the writing of a future "character":

James Boswell, a most amicable man. He improved and beautified his paternal estate of Auchinleck; made a distinguished figure in Parliament; had the honour to command a regiment of footguards, and was one of the brightest wits in the court of George the Third. (p. 181)

Amid this artifice and role playing we must not forget the dimension added by Johnston, who functions as Boswell's auditor. He receives periodic installments of the Journal and in addition to observing the events of the Journal observes Boswell self-consciously recounting those events. The manipulation and role playing in the London Journal is quite complex. What is particularly striking is the extent to which the roles do not seem to fit Boswell. Macheath was, after all, a jailed criminal. Mr. Spectator was an older, wiser, anonymous, Whiggish *observer*. Leaving aside the question of the brightness of the wits in George the Third's court, it is fair to say that Boswell has little in common with the Restoration court poets. The point is that these figures are not so much heroes to Boswell as they are part of the landscape of his essentially literary imagination. For Boswell, as for many of us, the world is most real when it is least mundane, and the London Journal explores Boswell's relationships with the mundane world in which he moves and the reified imaginative world in which he lives. Both interpenetrate, both affect one another, and Boswell's treatment of the workings of the real and the artificial in the London Journal are nearly always fascinating and sometimes extremely sophisticated.

The most important aspect of Boswellian artifice in the London Journal is the fact that it conveys an authentic sense of Boswell's character and personality. For all the shaping, the editing, and the manipulation we still feel (and properly so) that our sense of Boswell—the image of Boswell which is emerging— is a reliable one, a "real" one. As biographer, Boswell plays up the importance of facts and details; as autobiographer he demonstrates that the shaping of those materials is far more important than his theoretical framework would suggest and that the gray area of experience—the realm of dream, fantasy, and imagination—is more real and compelling than his vaunted facts. Boswellian autobiography is, for this reason, more successful than Boswellian biography, for the realm of dream, fantasy, and imagination is seldom accessible to the biographer. As Boswell writes in the epigraph which introduced this chapter, "It is amazing how much every thing depends on the state of our minds at the time, and how little the state of any one's mind is known to others." Given the importance of mental states, states that shift not only from year to year but also from moment to moment, how can Boswell hope to represent Johnson's experience with any degree of reliability? This, of course, is one of the crucial issues which Johnson treats in his comparison of autobiography with biography. Only the autobiographer knows his own mental states. One may infer prior mental states on the basis of actions and one may receive glimpses of mental states through writings, particularly personal writings, but the biographer is still at an enormous disadvantage here. Unfortunately, Boswell often glosses over this difficulty by "entering" Johnson's mind and recounting what he finds there. Very often he enters without announcing his presence and leads his readers to believe that his reporting of Johnson's thoughts is accurate and authentic. Some Boswellian "accounts" have even been quoted as Johnson's own statements ("Dine with Jack Wilkes, Sir! I'd as soon dine with Jack Ketch").

As I argued earlier, Boswell can be masterful in the exploiting of the life/art dichotomy. However, this nexus of techniques and themes demands the constant presence of control. If Boswell "enters" Johnson's mind—an essentially artistic activity—but suggests that his role is reportorial, control is lost. "Control" is far simpler when we are dealing with our own mental states or with those of fictional characters. It is far more difficult when we are "describing" the attitudes and thoughts of another. The activity is also dangerous, for an able writer like Boswell can bring us to the point where we are inured to the liberties which he takes and forget to question his practices. We begin to feel that Johnson must have been elevated at the sight of orthodox, Tory Oxford. At the dinner with Wilkes, Johnson's habitual muttering *must* be provoked by the obnoxious Arthur Lee's being not only a *patriot* but an *American.* Beyond question he comes to the table because he recollects "his having rated [Boswell] for supposing that he could be at all disconcerted by any company . . ." (*Life,* III, 68). It may be that Boswell's accounts are accurate. My point, however, is that Boswell's reliability turns on his ultimate sense of Johnson's mind and personality. He is guessing; the question concerns how educated those guesses are. Boswell's "image" of Johnson, despite Boswell's apparent attitude toward it, is of consummate importance. Boswell's shortcomings in understanding Johnson's politics, religion, and interest in science (the relation to man, God, and nature) are, I think, demonstrable. As I will argue later, there are other relationships on which Boswell is also shaky. The entering of Johnson's mind is a more difficult (and usually far more complex) task than Boswell's practices suggest, though Boswell's ability to mask this difficulty is a sign of his skill if not of his "perfect authenticity." His accounts of Johnson's thoughts may, indeed, be accurate, but the evidence concerning his awareness of the nature of Johnson's thought and attitudes is not such as to make us comfortable in this regard.

Another area where falsification can result from a lack of control is that of the biographer's point of view. Boswell is so adept at depicting scenes that one can easily forget the type and extent of coloring which he adds to those scenes. For example, he often allows his imaginative realm to become the arena for Johnson's actions. I will treat this in greater detail in the next chapter. Here I would only say that to place Johnson in Boswell's "world" is, very often, to graft attitudes and beliefs onto him which he either does not hold or has less interest in than Boswell does. It is important for us to see "Boswell's Johnson"—to see Johnson as a figure amid the personages, events, and locales in Boswell's memory—but it is most dangerous to forget the uniqueness and limitations of Boswell's point of view, of his method of seeing. We can illustrate this point by watching both men describe the same experience. Here is Johnson, in the *Journey*, describing their arrival at Rasay:

The boat was under the direction of Mr. Malcolm Macleod, a gentleman of Raasay. The water was calm, and the rowers were vigorous; so that our passage was quick and pleasant. When we came near the island, we saw the laird's house, a neat modern fabrick, and found Mr. Macleod, the proprietor of the island, with many gentlemen, expecting us on the beach. We had, as at all other places, some difficulty in landing. The craggs were irregularly broken, and a false step would have been very mischievous.

It seemed that the rocks might, with no great labour, have been hewn almost into a regular flight of steps; and as there are no other landing places, I considered this rugged ascent as the consequence of a form of life inured to hardships, and therefore not studious of nice accommodations. But I know not whether, for many ages, it was not considered as a part of military policy, to keep the country not easily accessible. The rocks are natural fortifications, and an enemy climbing with difficulty, was easily destroyed by those who stood high above him. (pp. 58-59)

Here, in severely abbreviated form, is Boswell:

We got into Rasay's *carriage*, which was a good strong open boat made in Norway. The wind had now risen pretty high, and was against us; but we had four stout rowers, particularly a Macleod, a robust, black-haired fellow, half naked, and bare-headed, something between a wild Indian and an English tar. Dr. Johnson sat high on the stern, like a magnificent Triton. . . . We sailed along the coast of Scalpa, a rugged island, about four miles in length. Dr. Johnson proposed that he and I should buy it, and found a good school, and an episcopal church, . . . and have a printing-press, where he would print all the Erse that could be found.

The approach to Rasay was very pleasing. We saw before us a beautiful bay, well defended by a rocky coast; a good family mansion; a fine verdure about it,—with a considerable number of trees;—and beyond it hills and mountains in gradation of wildness. Our boatmen sung with great spirit. Dr. Johnson observed, that naval musick was very ancient. As we came near the shore, the singing of our rowers was succeeded by that of reapers, who were busy at work, and who seemed

to shout as much as to sing, while they worked with a bounding activity. Just as we landed, I observed a cross, or rather the ruins of one,
upon a rock, which had to me a pleasing vestige of religion. (*Tour*, V,
162-65)

About 75 percent of Boswell's text is omitted; his treatment is far
more detailed than Johnson's and includes, among other things,
some interesting dialogue. Johnson's description is partially
bound by the purposes of his book, but it is still very
representative. It points up his "modernism," his curiosity, his
circumspect judgment, and insight in practical affairs. Boswell's
account is quite different. "Dr." Johnson is "like a magnificent
Triton," quoting Horace and speculating on the founding of an
episcopal church. The laird's house is a "good *family* mansion"
rather than a "neat modern fabrick" and this mansion is set in
nearly "feudal" environs. All around are happy workers. When
the rowers stop singing we hear the reapers (almost on cue, in
cinematic fashion). While Johnson's attention is focused on
rocks, his mind on rudeness, hardship, and "military policy,"
Boswell observes a ruined cross.

I am certainly not arguing that Boswell offers us lies. Boswell
provides us with very important information. However,
Boswell's vision of the scene in which Johnson is placed is a
subjective one, clearly affected by Boswell's romantic conservatism: his sense of family and tradition, his obsession with
certain aspects of religion and his quasi-feudalism. There is some
overlap of Johnson's and Boswell's attitudes but never as much
as Boswell would suggest. The cumulative result of passages
such as this—both in the *Tour* and in the *Life*—is the continual
association of Johnson with particular aspects of religious and
political conservatism. The result has been that we have had to
adjust our sense of Johnson's religion and politics and, to an
extent, rediscover those aspects of his personality exemplified,
for example, in the *Journey* passage cited, aspects which Boswell
often neglects. To use a novelistic analogy, Boswell's *Life*
ostensibly treats Johnson but it places Johnson in Boswell's
milieu and treats him from Boswell's point of view. The "central
consciousness" of the *Life* is Boswell's and not Johnson's. The

milieu, however, is so fully realized that we may not even be aware of the falsification involved in its deployment.

One must distinguish between falsification and "heightening." The stress of certain details and the conscious structuring of material to achieve effects is, of course, to be expected, although I am dubious of the practice of tampering with facts in the interest of achieving an account more "faithful" to the realities of the situation as perceived by the biographer. In any case, the ultimate test or measure concerns the biographer's "image" of his subject and its depth and sophistication. For example, Boswell's account of Johnson's interview with George III is frequently praised, but its presentation is not altogether accurate. Boswell presents the encounter as an event of solemnity and even mystery. Barnard "[steals] round to the apartment where the King was," lights his way through darkened rooms until George enters the library through a "private door . . . of which his Majesty had the key" (*Life*, II, 34). The keeper of the key meets the keeper of the book. Johnson is "in a profound study" and, after Barnard whispers "Sir, here is the King," rises. The talk which follows is often pedestrian, particularly after Boswell's masterful introduction of it. The introduction, however, is less than precise. The reader does not have the sense, for example, that there were others present in the library (which—as the Caldwell Minute makes clear—there were) or that George talked to others in the library (which he did). Such information would break Boswell's spell. For Boswell, this meeting is of great importance, but his method of presenting it "heightens" it to a degree that is as excessive as his introductory comment concerning Johnson's "monarchical enthusiasm" (*Life*, II, 33). Boswell's sense of Johnson's political orientation, the basis for the shaping, is imprecise and the result is undue manipulation and a false sense of setting. There is also a certain sadness in the scene. Obviously, an encounter with royalty is of immense importance to Boswell, but as we read through his later Journal his encounters with George III are nearly always unsatisfying. George's comments to Boswell are predictable (How long have you been in London? When are you returning to Scotland?) and they demonstrate that he tends to forget answers which he has received to such questions in the past. As I will argue later, the chief value of the *Life* is autobiographical, not biographical. The meeting of Johnson and the king is an event which Boswell nearly idealizes, because he never shares the excitement of that encounter. As such, it tells us a great deal about Boswell. It tells us far less about Johnson.

There is a subtler danger of falsification in Boswell's use of "scenes." As Molin and other have noted, Boswell himself lived in scenes ("Boswell's Account of the Johnson-Wilkes Meeting," p. 309). His life is a series of great encounters: with Voltaire, Rousseau, Paoli, and particularly Johnson. We think of him with Pitt, at Hume's deathbed, with Gaubius in Holland, with poor Reid, with Lord Marischal, Lord Mountstuart, Wilkes, Kames, Monboddo, Lord Hailes, the members of the Club, and of course with Temple, Grange, Erskine, Dempster, and Lord Eglinton. He measures himself against the character and personality of others. Throughout the early sections of his Journal he tells himself to "Be Auchinleck," to "Be Johnson." The best scenes in the *Life* often involve encounters as well. We think of Johnson with Wilkes, with George III, in the *Tour* with Flora Macdonald and with Lord Auchinleck. There is not necessarily any lying here or misrepresentation, but the cumulative effect of such scenes is to blind us to equally important, often more important aspects of Johnson's life. Johnson is, to an important extent, Boswellized. We may forget Johnson's encounters with books, with ideas, with events. He is presented, very often, in social contexts and we can easily come to think of him as we think of Boswell, a person who meets interesting and important people. To be sure, Johnson did meet such people, but I suspect such meetings were of far less importance to Johnson than similar events were to Boswell, and to think of Johnson in the context of personal encounters is, often, to blind ourselves to contexts of equal or greater importance.

Moreover, Boswell—like the Puritan biographers—is an inveterate allegorizer. Many of Johnson's encounters in the *Life* and *Tour* suggest large, conceptual jostlings:

Johnson-George III	king of letters and ruler of the political realm
	archetypal tory and the embodiment of his principles
Johnson-Wilkes	archetypal moralist and archetypal profligate
	archetypal defender of the *status quo* and archetypal radical
Johnson-Monboddo	monarch of common sense and epitome of rash speculation
Johnson-Flora Macdonald	theoretical Jacobite and practical Jacobite
Johnson-Lord Auchinleck	Tory and Whig
	Anglican and Presbyterian
	Englishman and Scotsman
	spiritual father and physical father (for Boswell)
Johnson-Boswell	Englishman and Scotsman
	self-made man and ancient Baron
	age and youth
	tutor and pupil
	moralist and sensualist
	physician and sick man
	surrogate father and surrogate son

The drama of many of these encounters is undeniable, even though it often results from Boswellian embroidery. One problem, as I just indicated, is that we are presented with a contextual approach to Johnson which may dull our awareness of certain other relevant contexts. There are two additional dangers. The presentation of a character in terms that are larger than life can easily lead to stereotyping and caricature. Moreover, the attractions of allegorizing may blind us to the fact that certain participants may in fact *not* embody the position or notion they are made to represent. A technique that should clarify may in fact obfuscate. Finally, the encounters in which we find Johnson have sometimes been determined by Boswell— the social catalyst—and they often reflect his interests far more than Johnson's. There were meetings of which we would surely prefer to know more, for example, Johnson's meeting with Franklin. I am also sure that Boswell hesitated to report certain encounters in detail (or failed to enquire concerning them) simply because he lacked interest. One thinks here, for example, of Johnson's dealings with manufacturers, technologists, and inventors. This really brings us to the larger question of the contexts in which Johnson is defined, the subject of the next chapter.

CHAPTER IV

The Question of Setting

I had a full relish of life today. It was somehow like being in London in the last age. I felt myself of some real personal consequence while I made one of such a company. . . . (Boswell for the Defence, p. 107)

B oswell records an important distinction of Johnson's concerning what he terms "physical and moral truth":

Physical truth is when you tell a thing as it really subsists in itself; moral truth is when you tell a thing sincerely and precisely as it appears to you. I say such a one walked across the street. If he really did so it was physical truth. If I thought so, though I should have been mistaken, it was Moral Truth. (*Corr—Life*, p. 358)

In the contexts of eighteenth-century science and philosophy one can only "tell a thing as it really subsists in itself" in a loose, practical sense. Telling a thing "sincerely and precisely as it appears to you" is not a rigorous activity either, for feelings are to an important extent dependent on language for their expression so that one-to-one equivalency between "appearance" and "telling" is impossible. However, that "appearance" is of critical importance for eighteenth-century thought and should be of equal importance for the eighteenth-century biographer. His major problem is that noted in the previous chapter, the inaccessibility of another's mind. Boswell describes Adams' impression of Johnson at Pembroke College as beloved, gay, and happy as "a striking proof of the fallacy of appearances, and how little any of us know of the real internal state even of those whom we see most frequently . . . " (*Life,* I, 73). Boswell's judgment is all well and good, but it does not suggest a way out of the biographer's dilemma—facing the insoluble problem of the private nature of mental experience, how does the biographer minimize the falsification of his biographical subject? Answers are possible but they are usually easier to give than to apply. For example, mental states affect the setting in which they occur just as the setting may induce certain states. As I commented above, such relationships involve an interaction which cannot be neatly interrupted. The result is that the biographer cannot talk of setting without talking of the individual psychology of his biographical subject. It would be silly, for example, to argue that Johnson would probably be comforted by a pastoral locale because pastoral locales are comforting to nearly all other people. Instead, one must infer mental states in discrete situations or settings from a general sense of the unique biographical subject, a sense based on an examination and weighing of all available evidence. (Johnson says this of pastoral poets, of travel writers, and landscape architects. . . . When Johnson was in France he expressed a desire to see. . . . In Johnson's letters there are continual references to such favorite places as. . . . Johnson's library contains many books on . . . but very few on. . . . In his own writings Johnson seldom refers to landscape in . . . contexts. In conversation Johnson was particularly engaged by the introduction of such subjects as. . . . None of the accounts of Johnson by those who knew him include discussions of Johnson's possible interest in. . . . etc. Thus, his reaction to this locale was *probably* one of . . . and his comment that ". . . " should *probably* be taken seriously.)

Again, it is the "image" which is important, an image distilled from all the evidence at the biographer's disposal, an image which aids in the process of educated guesswork. We have seen its importance in several areas; it is equally important when one attempts to describe the biographical subject contextually. I use the word "setting" in a broad sense, though certain specific senses should also come to mind. In commenting on the factors which determine character, William L. Howarth mentions sense of self (to be treated in the next chapter), sense of place, of history, and of the motivation for writing ("Some Principles of Autobiography," p. 365). Goethe treats similar issues; his comments here are suggestive:

For the principal task of biography, I believe, is to present a man in the condition of his time, and to show to what extent those conditions, taken as a whole, thwart him or favor him, how he forms from it all a view of the world and of men, and how, if he is an artist, a poet, or a writer, he then takes that view and projects it back into the world. It is, however, an almost impossible task, for what is demanded is that the individual know both himself and his century—himself insofar as he has remained the same in all circumstances, the century inasmuch as it sweeps both the willing and the unwilling along with it, determining and forming them, so that it can truthfully be said that any man, had he been born a mere ten years earlier or later, might, as far as his own formation and his outward achievements are concerned, have become an entirely different person. (*Autobiography*, I, 2c)

Indeed Goethe sets a difficult task, one even more difficult for the biographer than the autobiographer, for he must know the biographical subject and his century as well as himself and his relationship to that century, so that falsification of the biographical subject may be minimized. Johnson, his century and his works, not to mention Boswell, his century, and his works, are a very large subject. Thus I can only hope to suggest the outline of an answer to the problems raised by Goethe. In general, I think that one of the chief difficulties with the *Life* is that Johnson, all too often, is placed in a Boswellian setting. Johnson's own sense of setting is both more particular and more general than Boswell's. Johnson measures himself against eternal norms and sees his life in an eternal context. Boswell may share Johnson's religious orientation in this regard but he is far more involved with mundane relationships—land, class, titles, social company—and tends to measure himself against individuals rather than against spiritual norms. Johnson is more concerned with the imitation of Christ, Boswell with the imitation of Johnson. Moreover, Boswell's interest in his personal affairs often overrides his interest in public ones. Johnson's concern with concrete contemporary issues is often overlooked as Boswell focuses on matters of interest to himself. Thus we receive interminable passages detailing his consultation of Johnson with regard to legal cases in process and yet have little sense, for example, of the political backdrop in which Johnson is very much involved. Who, upon reading the *Life*, would have any full sense of the occurrence and importance of the Seven Years' War and of Johnson's rigorous opposition to it? Yet all are subjected to discussions of trivial matters relieved only by quotable Johnsonian statements, some of them chastizing Boswell for inquiring concerning such issues.

Tinker remarks that Boswell's Johnson is conceived "as the hero of a drama of almost national proportions" (*Young Boswell*, p. 225), but Pottle sees an important degree of falsification in Boswell's sense of Johnson as an alternative to the kind of world which emerges after his death:

We forget . . . unless we read the journal, that the "Life" was written and published in the awful shadow of the French Revolution. No man was ever more robust in his sympathies or more tolerant of opposed opinion than Boswell in his best years, but the "Life" contains a distressing number of stiff and angry notes, the object of which is not so much to affirm his own political and religious orthodoxy as to insult those who differ with him. He was terrified at what might happen and no longer had the energy to repel his fears. Had the "Life" been written ten years earlier, hardly one of those extravagantly Tory passages which gave Macaulay his animus would have been in it.[1]

It is an interesting question to ask whether or not Johnson's likely reaction to the French Revolution could be inferred, based

1. Frederick A. Pottle, "The Life of Boswell," p. 453. It should be noted, in this connection, that the bulk of the rough draft of the *Life* was written from September 1786 to May 1788 (*PP*, XVII, i-ii). The "horrid scenes in France" to which Boswell refers in 1792 (*PP*, XVIII, 160) would not have an impact then. In this regard, see also Irma S. Lustig, "Boswell on Politics in *The Life of Johnson*," p. 390.

on the sense of Johnson's politics and social awareness which emerges in the *Life*, but, as Goethe points out, the events in France would affect Johnson's character and it would be misleading to discuss his possible reaction to an event in the light of his known "character," a character unaffected by that event. Looking in the opposite direction, with Goethe, it is interesting to speculate on the possible course of Johnson's career and the pattern of his work had he arrived in London ten years earlier. His relationships to Pope and Swift, for example, might have been quite different. Iffy questions may be useful ones just as they may be silly; my point is that Boswell seldom poses interesting ones. It is better to have Johnson's response to the possibility of being locked up with an infant than not to have it, but searching questions concerning possible relationships with major intellectual, literary, or political figures would be more valuable. It is, of course, easy in retrospect to throttle Boswell in our imaginations ("Why didn't you ask Johnson about this; you had the chance and we do not?"). In fairness, we must contrast those questions which Boswell asked (and the answers which he recorded) with the paucity of material left by his predecessors and contemporaries. Boswell may fall far short of ideal norms but what he has left far exceeds the contributions of his competitors. It is equally important, however, to constantly keep in mind the disparity between Boswell's interests and Johnson's. We must guard against the assumption that an often Boswellized Johnson is instead a Johnson who has been preserved with perfect authenticity.

Biographers present their subjects in a number of contexts. Some depend on the interests of the biographer, some on the pattern of the biographical subject's experience, and some on common human tendencies and common literary principles. The limitations of Boswell's notions of context are striking, although they are partially explicable in historical terms, partially explicable in personal ones. In a sense, for example, it is unfair to require of Boswell an advanced understanding and use of "milieu," for as Paul Korshin comments, "the introduction of the milieu concept is a big step in biography, one which does not mature until the later eighteenth century."[2] However, we must remember that in the case of judgments such as this we should approach the *Life* not as a rude bit of generic groping but as the book which is most frequently adjudged the greatest biography of all times. The book's importance justifies the most searching criticism. Moreover, I am not persuaded that genres always evolve from primitive experiment to polished triumph. In the case of the novel and of the periodical essay, for example, eighteenth-century writers often seem to have comprehended the possibilities and limits of the genres from the beginning. In the case of *Tristram Shandy* and the *Rambler*, for example, those possibilities and limits are thematically central to the works themselves. Why then is it not reasonable to expect a parallel level of sophistication in eighteenth-century biography?

Contexts may be avoided for a number of reasons. One context on which Boswell is particularly weak is that of Johnson's sexual relationships. He is able to write the tasteless verses on Johnson's impending nuptials with Mrs. Thrale, but he cannot provide detailed accounts of this aspect of Johnson's experience. Some material was simply suppressed, for example, the information concerning Johnson's fondling of Mrs. Desmoulins and his contemplation of a second marriage. Here we are dealing with falsification and Boswell is demonstrably culpable. Clearly, however, there are sexual aspects of Johnson's experience which Boswell could not reasonably be expected to treat. It would be absurd to expect of Boswell a detailed account and explanation of something like the chains and padlock business with Mrs. Piozzi. We must understand such matters, however, if only to avoid some of the speculation which is itself often grounded on earlier speculation. Moreover, the armchair psychoanalysis which Bernard DeVoto deplored in literary commentators may often be found in discussions of Johnson.

2. Paul J. Korshin, "*Ana*-Books and Intellectual Biography in the Eighteenth Century," p. 193. Cf. Korshin's discussion (p. 196) of the perfunctory nature of the "character" usually included in eighteenth-century biographies: "Even in the most elaborate works, these are usually confined to discussions of personality traits or the listing of literary accomplishments. Seldom do we find analyses of intellectual qualities."

(We are sometimes told, for example, that Johnson's vigorous eating habits represented a displacement of sexual desire; one appetite was satisfied when the other could not be.) It is quite likely that Johnson's sexual experience, once detailed and studied to the extent possible, would aid us in explaining other facets of his experience. It is almost certain that his sexual habits (as presently "understood") do not explain all that they have been made to explain.

Boswell was not ignorant of the importance of sex for the life-writer. He knew that importance from personal experience and demonstrates his awareness of it in his autobiographical writings. Moreover, he had available to him judgments such as Bayle's that the primary causal factor in historical events is situated between the knee and the navel. It is fair to say that Boswell's audience—which was sometimes shaken by the revelation of private conversations and correspondence—would have to be treated with extreme delicacy, but—as the nineteenth-century novelists ably demonstrate—delicacy and sexual intensity may coexist very nicely. Boswell need not have avoided these matters in the way that he did. In my judgment, Donald Greene's argument that Boswell simply could not cope with a "human" Johnson is persuasive. Perhaps it would have been better had Boswell avoided the issue completely, for when he does approach it the result is a general discussion which really tells us nothing but suggests anything and everything:

In short, it must not be concealed, that, like many other good and pious men, among whom we may place the Apostle Paul upon his own authority, Johnson was not free from propensities which were ever "warring against the law of his mind,"—and that in his combats with them, he was sometimes overcome. (*Life,* IV, 396)

If Boswell has any evidence for his statement he is careful to shield us from it. The illustration which Boswell does give of Johnson's "uncommonly strong and impetuous" amorous inclinations is his practice of interviewing prostitutes. We may now observe such activities on daytime as well as nighttime television and inspect detailed accounts that are sandwiched between recipes and household-hint sections of "women's" magazines. If this is evidence of impetuosity and excessive libido, the emotions are rather common. At any rate, we need have no "common" feelings concerning Johnson for we are to think of him as another St. Paul.

The two relationships to which Boswell gives his primary attention are Johnson's relation to his God and to his country— Johnson's religion and politics—and Boswell is imprecise in both areas. I will not belabor points which have been made time and again, but only say that it is perilous to approach Boswell on Johnson's politics and religion without studying the commentaries of Professors Voitle, Quinlan, Chapin, and Greene. Boswell's weak account of these matters results both from ignorance and from conscious manipulation. He is also weak on relationships which are more personal than ideological. He has little of interest to say, for example, on Johnson's relationships with his parents and brother, and, as has always been pointed out, he is generally weak on the events of Johnson's youth. Clifford's biography is here indispensable and Irwin's discussions of Johnson's relationship with his mother suggest whole areas of experience (and repercussions for Johnson's works) which one looks for in vain in the *Life.*

It is of course unfair to require modern psychoanalysis in the *Life.* It is not unreasonable, however, to expect a careful reading of Johnson's works and a realization of the extent to which so many passages in those works are autobiographical. Many have followed Boswell in interpreting Johnson's personality and experience without consulting Johnson himself, the one individual closest to those matters and one who discusses them almost constantly. Johnson also refers in his works to his wife, his family, friends, and acquaintances. Mrs. Piozzi was not alone in her awareness of this fact but even today relatively little has been done with it.

Boswell does treat Johnson in relation to his times but not in ways that would even begin to satisfy Goethe's norms. There is also some discussion of Johnson's relation to nature (both in his scientific interests and in his views of landscape) but Boswell is thin here. What is distressing is that he is also thin on the relation of Johnson to his works. We may be indebted to Boswell for information concerning such matters as time of composition, rapidity of composition, financial arrangements with booksellers, and the public reception of Johnson's works (when Boswell is accurate) but we seldom get much more than this. As a reader of Johnson's works, Boswell has sometimes had his defenders, but in my judgment he is neither sophisticated nor assiduous in this regard. His list of Johnson's prose works is unreliable; he sometimes reveals that he has not inspected with care the works which he mentions. He does make interesting comments from time to time but so do, for example, Mrs. Piozzi and Arthur Murphy.

More interesting perhaps is Boswell's treatment of Johnson's relation to his books and to his work.[3] Boswell does not, for example, use the sale catalogue of Johnson's library although it would have been available to him. The student who confronts the catalogue after a long sojourn with Boswell is immediately struck by the extent and variety of the material there and is suddenly able to challenge numerous silly arguments and assumptions concerning Johnson's attitudes, "prejudices," and interests. To an important extent Johnson's reading has been Boswellized. We tend to think of him in the context of a few key works: with Law altering his religious life, for example, or with Burton drawing him from bed in the morning. However, it is Boswell who so often reads in this fashion. He is impressionable and easily swayed. He reads enthusiastically (in, to a degree, the eighteenth-century sense of the word) and allows his reading to impinge directly on his everyday life. ("My misery is that, like my friend Dempster, I am convinced by the last book which I have read" [*Boswell in Holland*, p. 252].) There are, in the *Life*, many references to Johnson's wide reading and specific works are mentioned, but there is always the lingering impact of that

3. See Korshin's "An Unrecovered World: Samuel Parr's Projected Life of Johnson" for a discussion of the qualifications necessary to trace Johnson's intellectual life. See also Donald Greene's important introduction to his recent edition of the sale catalogue of Johnson's library.

statement, "It is a sad reflection, but a true one, that I knew almost as much at eighteen as I do now" (*Life*, I, 445), a statement which is qualified, of course, but latently suggests that Johnson the conversationalist is *the* Johnson, drawing on reserves stored long ago. This *judgment* can be countered by using the *Life* but it is difficult to do away with the *impression*.

Moreover, the thought of Johnson's actually working with books with a degree of intensity that, in John Wain's judgment, brought him "to a state bordering on breakdown" (*Samuel Johnson*, p. 193) is unsettling. It is far easier to think of him in romantic fashion, balancing on his broken chair, stirring up dust that has accumulated on recondite tomes, giving directions to servants concerning his accessibility, taking a break now and then with his distillation apparatus. Wain's treatment of Johnson at work, like Clifford's very useful discussion ("Some Aspects of London Life in the Mid-18th Century") of such matters as the quotidian vicissitudes of life in Johnson's residence—the problems of water and of sanitation, for example—are very important correctives to Boswell. John Drinkwater comments on the solitary Johnson. Such an artist, he writes,

is of necessity very largely a lonely man, living apart through a great deal of his time in meditation, his mind discovering itself almost in secrecy, or stimulated not by easy contact with many others, but by some deep fusion with one or two. It is of this side of Johnson, which must have been there, that we get little suggestion in Boswell's vivid pages. (*The Muse in Council*, p. 218)

"Shining in good company," Drinkwater points out, "is a small thing when set beside the greater imaginative achievement which, after all, was Johnson's life-long hope and endeavour" (p. 220). Elizabeth Bruss (*Autobiographical Acts*, p. 72) comments, very cogently, that "Boswell writes not to capture the 'being' of Johnson but the experience of 'being with' him. He is therefore little concerned with rendering the content of Johnson's consciousness; we learn nothing, in fact, of the subjective life of Johnson that does not appear in his own memoranda."

Boswell's romantic perspective on himself and on Johnson

with regard to work is quite remarkable. In 1764 (*Boswell in Holland*, pp. 162-68) he recounts his plan to produce a Scots dictionary. What ultimately appeals to him is the possibility of an opportunity to be cast in a particular role:

I confess that I look forward some centuries from now and see with romantic pleasure the Scots of that day applying themselves to the study of their ancient tongue as to Greek or Latin, and considering themselves much indebted to the work of Old Boswell, who has made it possible for them to taste the excellent works of their brave, happy, and venerable ancestors. . . . (p. 165)

Fusty "Old Boswell," embalmed on a library shelf, a mediator between the future and the idyllic past: Boswell abandoned the project but not the attitudes which coalesce in his comments on it. Because he mediates for us in the *Life* it is often difficult to remember the Johnson of the preface to *his* Dictionary and all of the experience which precedes the crucial account of the sickness and sorrow surrounding the project. Boswell refers to that pain in his character of Johnson, but it is easy to romanticize that pain, especially in the case of Dictionary Johnson, "well arm'd like a hero of yore," flailing the French and even pausing from his heroic endeavor to twit the Scots, the pensioners, and the excisemen.

The only context with which Boswell is really taken is the social context; his "Johnson" is best displayed in conversation among his friends. This is probably the image which most readily comes to mind when the *Life* is mentioned. Brooks's comment is appropriate:

The *Life of Samuel Johnson* is no life and times, for it affords only sporadic treatments of background events. . . . Boswell's biography of Johnson is, rather, a great stage over which pass many of the distinguished literary personalities of Johnson's time, either as personages or as subjects of conversations. (*James Boswell*, p. 120)

The London Journal is of immense importance in this regard, for it points up the importance of social life to Boswell and the manner in which certain facets of social life are part and parcel of his imaginative landscape. One of the most important repeating roles in the London Journal (along with the role of Macheath) is that which associates Boswell with Mr. Spectator:

As we drove along and spoke good English, I was full of rich imagination of London, ideas suggested by the Spectator and such as I could not explain to most people, but which I strongly feel and am ravished with. My blood glows and my mind is agitated with felicity. (p. 130)

I wrought myself up to the imagination that it was the age of Sir Richard Steele, and that I was like him sitting in judgment on a new comedy. (p. 177)

Between five and six we set out. I imagined myself the Spectator taking one of his rural excursions. (p. 244)

At three o'clock I went to Westminster Abbey. . . . I recalled the ideas of it which I had from *The Spectator*. (p. 270)

Temple and I drank coffee at *Will's*, so often mentioned in *The Spectator*. (p. 286)

The importance of the *Spectator* for eighteenth-century thought is difficult to exaggerate. It simultaneously served as an entrée into certain facets of English manners and culture, a distillation of central themes in science, aesthetics, and epistemology, a hortatory manual, and—in its own right—as a work of art, the preeminent example of a new genre (actually an amalgam of earlier genres but still sufficiently "new" as to generate legions of imitators in its own mold), a work which continually appears, for example, in the private libraries of students of things English—an indispensable text in this regard. For Boswell it is all these things and more; it is, quintessentially, London, Boswell's (as Johnson points out) nearly obsessive love ("Why, Sir, I never knew any one who had such a *gust* for London as you have . . ." [*Life*, III, 176]). In 1783 Boswell writes to Grange:

Some time or other I flatter myself I shall go over the classical scenes of London with you and revive the finest ideas of our younger years which the *Spectator* gave us. (*Corr—Grange*, p. 298)

The *Beggar's Opera* serves a similar function in that it continually "revives London ideas" for Boswell. He refers to it constantly in his Journal, attends performances of it whenever possible, and even considered editing it. Boswell's love of London generates, in my judgment, a number of problems. In the first place, Mr. Spectator's London is not Johnson's. As we read Boswell we telescope the time frame and can easily forget the fact that a young man's search for Mr. Spectator's London in the 1760s is not altogether unlike a young man's search in the New York of today for the New York of Scott Fitzgerald. The crucial difference is that many *Spectator* associations did in fact (and do) still exist and that the changes in London over the approximately fifty year period were, though real, not staggering. The expansion of population, of traffic, and of the metropolis itself were quite real, as was the fact of London's growing position as the headquarters of world banking and credit. Changes in hygiene and in other facets of life are also demonstrable, but London had not altered so significantly as my New York parallel. Still, the days of Anne, of the Tory satirists, of the Union (unmarred by the events of 1715 and 1745) were no more. What is chiefly important in my parallel is the young man and the position in his imaginative life of literary fixtures:

The truth is that *imaginary* London, gilded with all the brilliancy of warm fancy as I have viewed it, and London as a scene of real business, are quite different; and as the *changes* of fanciful sensation are very painful, it is more comfortable to have the duller sensation of reality. (*PP*, XVI, 159)

This statement was made, not in 1762, but in January 1786. A month later (p. 166) Boswell wrote in his Journal, "How humiliating is it that I am so much under the dominion of fancy!"

Boswell places Johnson in his, Boswell's, London, and this is a source of great pleasure in the *Life*, for Johnson is the epitome of London for Boswell, a London of wit, intelligence, and conversation, and Boswell's affection for this setting and its greatest fixture informs and enlivens his work. It also, however, falsifies Johnson, for Johnson's London is that of Hogarth as well as of Mr. Spectator, a London in which, for example, the activities of the middle class do not dominate our attention. Johnson loves

London but through realistic eyes. Boswell goes to London as to a shrine which houses a living saint:

Though then but two-and-twenty, I had for several years read [Johnson's] works with delight and instruction, and had the highest *reverence* for their authour, which had grown up in my fancy into a kind of mysterious *veneration*, by figuring to myself a state of *solemn* elevated abstraction, in which I supposed him to live in the immense metropolis of London. (*Life*, I, 383-84)

[referring to the address of Davies' shop]: No. 8.—The very place where I was fortunate enough to be introduced to the illustrious subject of this work, deserves to be particularly marked. I never pass by it without feeling *reverence* and regret. (*Life*, I, 390n; my italics throughout)

Boswell's feelings for London are easy to understand. The contrast, for example, between Edinburgh and London is striking and points up important dimensions of Boswell's personality. Edinburgh is dark and imposing, famous in eighteenth-century Europe for the height of its buildings, and made up very often of a system of constricting closes; the old town—in which Boswell grew up—looms above you and both topographically and architecturally suggests the power of religion, law, and public opinion which a man like Boswell could only see as cloying and threatening. It is a vertical city from which Boswell seeks escape. Thus, as he constantly points out in his Journal, he is happiest on Arthur's Seat. There he is free and he is in a romantic setting, despite the proximity of Arthur's Seat to the heart of the city. He can view the town and the Firth; he is in control. London, on the other hand, is a horizontal city, and Boswell is quite willing to traverse much of it daily. In the London Journal, for example, we find him lodging in Downing Street (in view of the Footguards) but frequenting Child's coffee-house in St. Paul's Church-Yard. London provides Boswell anonymity (when he seeks it) as well as the opportunity for donning multiple guises and playing multiple roles. It is an absolutely crucial part of his intellectual and emotional life and his failure to establish a successful practice when he finally succeeded in moving to London is especially poignant. In 1781 Boswell writes to Reynolds: "The truth is that in this dull northern town, I am not the same Man that you see in the Metropolis. I have not that jocund complacency that eager gayety which you have frequently cherished" (*Corr—Club*, p. 113). The days of role playing and sexual frolics may have largely passed at this point, but the disparity between Edinburgh and social London is apparent.

Boswell's London, however, is not Johnson's. It excludes too many things and places too much stress on a single facet of experience. It would be excessive to speak of Boswell as possessing a "coffee-house" or "club" vision of experience but it is accurate, I think, to argue that in certain social contexts Boswell's values coalesce. He achieves a kind of stasis and, if only momentarily, catches glimpses of a correlative for his private world of romantic dreams:

There is, I am sorry to say, an almost total extinction of one noble principle, which in the last age was to be found amongst all but men lost to decency and virtue. I mean the principle of *loyalty*. However old fashioned this principle may be at present, it is a worthy principle in whatever view it is regarded. But even at court, though I see much external *obeisance*, I do not find congenial sentiments to warm my heart; and except when I have the conversation of a very few select friends, I am never so well, as when I sit down to a dish of coffee in the Cocoa-Tree[4] sacred of old to loyalty, look around me to men of ancient families, and please myself with the consolatory thought that there is perhaps more good in the nation than I know. (*Hypochondriack*, I, 248-49)

To place Johnson in this world is to Boswellize him: to exaggerate certain contexts in which Johnson did move while playing down or excluding others, to exaggerate certain traits or attitudes or activities of Johnson while playing down or excluding others. The setting is Boswell's and as I argued earlier, the result is a book about Johnson but a book in which crucial

---

4. "A coffee-house frequented by the Tories; it gave its name to a club of Jacobites shortly before the Old Pretender's attempt to force his claims in 1715."—Margery Bailey's note, p. 249.

attitudes and points of view are those of Johnson's biographer. The setting tells us a great deal about Boswell and helps to solidify our sense of *Boswell's* Johnson, of all that Johnson meant and exemplified. The deftness and even fervor of its presentation, however, tends to mask the falsification which it engenders. When the function of setting in the *Life* is realized, the disparity between Boswell's Johnson and Johnson's Johnson becomes more apparent. Johnson's Johnson may or may not be of more help than Boswell's but to that Johnson we must now turn.

CHAPTER V

Johnson's Johnson

Nothing paints a truly great Man in Colours that strike the Eyes of the discerning Mind with more Energy, and captivating Force, than a Confession of his Weakness from his own Mouth. (Life of Boerhaave)

Boswell acknowledges the validity of Johnson's preference for autobiography over biography but justifies his own endeavors by pointing out that Johnson's autobiographical comments are scattered and fragmentary. Implicitly, the desultory labors of Johnson are contrasted with the assiduity of Boswell, the "persevering diligence" upon which Boswell prides himself and upon which he stakes his claims as biographer:

Had Dr. Johnson written his own life, in conformity with the opinion which he has given, that every man's life may be best written by himself; had he employed in the preservation of his own history, that clearness of narration and elegance of language in which he has embalmed so many eminent persons, the world would probably have had the most perfect example of biography that was ever exhibited. But although he at different times, in a desultory manner, committed to writing many particulars of the progress of his mind and fortunes, he never had persevering diligence enough to form them into a regular composition. Of these materials a few have been preserved; but the greater part was consigned by him to the flames, a few days before his death. (*Life*, I, 25)

We shall never know the precise nature of the materials which Johnson burned. Of the materials which remain, certain things may be said. The fragment which Johnson probably termed "Annals" was not seen by Boswell although it fully vindicates Boswell's judgment of the likely nature of an extended Johnsonian autobiography. It is, in its way, superior to anything in Boswell's *Life*. Its details are vivid, touching, and extremely suggestive. The fragment abounds in quotable passages (some involving dialogue) which provide striking insights into the nature of Johnson's family and his early life with them. It should be reread whenever one is on the verge of lavishing praise on Boswell, for it indicates what we might have had.

In a sense the practices which Johnson follows in his "Annals" conflict with an aspect of his biographical theory which Boswell utilizes. Much has been made of the cumulative pattern of Boswell's *Life*. Because Boswell assumes a relatively static notion of personality his task is to collect specimens of the various aspects of Johnson's personality. He is not obliged to weight his materials equally and he is not obliged to give equal attention to each year of Johnson's life. This notion of personality, child-as-father-of-man, justifies the structure of the *Life* and allows Boswell—with individual specimens or within individual scenes—to transcend temporal constraints and refer to earlier or later events or pronouncements.[1] Moreover, as I just indicated, Boswell has Johnsonian precedent for this view of personality; he appropriately cites Johnson's *Life of Sydenham* in this regard.[2] This view of personality conflicts with the well-known comments of Hume concerning the nature of identity. Hume, of course, argues that identity *per se* does not exist. There is no static identity to which we may point, for we inhabit a world of

1. See Alkon, "Boswellian Time"; David L. Passler, *Time, Form, and Style in Boswell's "Life of Johnson."*

2. *Life*, I, 38: "In following so very eminent a man from his cradle to his grave, every minute particular, which can throw light on the progress of his mind, is interesting. That he was remarkable, even in his earliest years, may easily be supposed; for to use his own words in his Life of Sydenham, . . . 'there is no instance of any man, whose history has been minutely related, that did not in every part of life discover the same proportion of intellectual vigour.' " Cf.

constant change and our identity is perforce the sum of all our experience at a particular moment. If one is to describe identity one must (as Johnson does in his "Annals") examine the stores of memory, for it is there that "identity" resides. In short, if one is to examine another's personality he must have a detailed sense of the experiences—and the associations attending them—of the biographical subject. Boswell's ignorance of this kind of information, particularly concerning Johnson's youth, severely limits his ability to understand Johnson's personality. I am not criticizing Boswell here, only pointing out the constraints within which he was forced to work.

The stores of memory represent somewhat intractable material even for the autobiographer for there is no way that he can present those materials to his reader in all of their fullness. This is part of the point of *Tristram Shandy*, of course. The autobiographer, like the biographer, is forced to shape his materials and present an image of the self, built of selected details though based on a knowledge of all details. Thus Hume's "My Own Life" is essentially a character, not an autobiography. Gibbon's *Memoirs* is an elaborate labor of self-love which involves highly conscious shaping and the most carefully considered utilization of phrase, detail, and scene.

It is useful, doubtless, to record experience in varied fashion so that the complexities of detail and the shaping of detail are apparent. Thus Johnson, for example, writes the "Annals" but also the *Prayers and Meditations*, which record responses to patterns of experience of a different order and—in their temporal dimension—of a different rhythm. Then too, there are passages suggesting the concerns of account books and appointment calendars as well as the detailed, clinical "Aegri

---

Life of Savage, p. 8: "There is reason to conjecture, that his Application was equal to his Abilities, because his Improvement was more than proportioned to the Opportunities, which he enjoyed; nor can it be doubted, that if his early Productions had been preserved, like those of happier Students, we might in some have found Sallies of that sprightly Humour, which distinguishes the *Author to be let*, and in others, Touches of that vigorous Imagination which painted the solemn scenes of *the Wanderer*."

Ephemeris." Boswell does this sort of thing himself, moving from notes to journal to literary text, from detailed jottings to finished characters and self-portraits. Some records are nearly clinical, some highly artificial and involving elaborate literary devices. But Johnson also indulged in self-portraiture and it is here that Boswell is open to criticism. Autobiographical passages abound in Johnson's works and, in my judgment, the self-portraits follow a discernible pattern, one of which Boswell is aware but one which he does not fully utilize. Boswell could not have access to *all* information on Johnson and it is both unrealistic and unfair to expect him to examine all *available* information, some of which it has taken centuries to fully recover. My concern is with Boswell's reluctance (or failure) to use materials which were readily available. If I am correct, the ultimate weakness of the *Life* is its lack of a coherent, sophisticated "image" of Johnson, an image based on all readily available details, an image which would enable Boswell to shape his materials in such a way as to present a reasonably reliable sense of the personality and character of his biographical subject. Within his own works Johnson provides such an image.

"Boswell's Johnson" is defended in strange ways. While acknowledging the fact that every portrait will be affected by subjective coloring—there is no image that is truly final—it is curious that Boswell's is defended on such grounds as longevity and popular acceptance. Johnson's Johnson, the Johnson nearly always forgotten in this type of discussion, is potentially of far greater importance than any of its competitors. It is not an elaborately detailed image but its simplicity is a crucial part of the conception itself. At any rate, it tells us much more than the fact that Johnson was both great and good.

The personal dimension of Johnson's works has not been overlooked. We know, for example, on Mrs. Piozzi's authority, that Johnson portrayed friends and acquaintances in his periodical essays (*Anecdotes*, p. 179). She also contends that "many of the severe reflections on domestic life in Rasselas, took their source from its author's keen recollections of the time passed in his early years," and that Johnson had his own mother in mind when he described peaceful old age in ll. 291-98 of *The*

Vanity of Human Wishes (Anecdotes, pp. 150-51). On John Nichols' authority, Tom Restless of *Idler* 48 has long been associated with Thomas Tyers; Hawkins claims that *Idler* 41 was occasioned by the death of Johnson's mother, and Bertrand Bronson has argued that Aspasia in *Irene* is an idealized portrait of Johnson's wife (*Johnson Agonistes and Other Essays,* pp. 137-40). Many general discussions in Johnson's works—of the plight of authors in the periodical essays, of the student in *The Vanity of Human Wishes,* for example—are of compelling personal significance. Boswell points out what he perceives (sometimes correctly, sometimes not) to be traces of Johnson's own personality in the *Lives of the Poets* (*Life,* IV, 45, 55). The sense of personal urgency is beyond question in a passage such as Johnson's discussion of the outset of Shakespeare's career:

He came to London a needy adventurer, and lived for a time by very mean employments. Many works of genius and learning have been performed in states of life, that appear very little favourable to thought or to enquiry; so many, that he who considers them is inclined to think that he sees enterprise and perseverance predominating over all external agency, and bidding help and hindrance vanish before them. The genius of Shakespeare was not to be depressed by the weight of poverty, nor limited by the narrow conversation to which men in want are inevitably condemned. . . . (*Johnson on Shakespeare,* VII, 88-89)

In his early biographical sketch of Lewis Morin, the French botanist and physician (1741), Johnson views the slow advance but eventual triumph of "unassisted merit" (1825 *Works,* VI, 393). There is now general agreement that one of Johnson's most important models was Boerhaave, the Dutch physician whose life he wrote in 1739. Catholic in his interests, modest but firm in the company of the great, subject to numerous forms of physical suffering, Boerhaave's personality and experience closely parallel Johnson's. He too began in poverty, "but with a Resolution equal to his Abilities, and a Spirit not to be depress'd or shaken, he determin'd to break thro' the Obstacles of Poverty, and supply by Diligence the want of Fortune."[3]

3. Robert James, *A Medicinal Dictionary* . . . (London, 1743, 1745), I, sig. 9Ulv.

It is natural, in such passages as these, to stress Johnson's need for inspiration, reassurance, and constant bolstering, for the self-portrait with which most of us are most fully acquainted is the Johnson of the *Prayers and Meditations:* the tormented individual, resolving to retard his backsliding, determined to rise early, keep a journal, read through scripture annually, and avoid idleness and sloth. Such self-disparagement is an important part of Johnson's process of self-examination. He told Mrs. Piozzi "that the character of *Sober* in the Idler, was . . . intended as his own portrait; and that he had his own outset into life in his eye when he wrote the eastern story of Gelaleddin" (*Anecdotes,* p. 178). *Idler* 31 begins with the suggestion that although pride enjoys the "pre-eminence of mischief" idleness provides pride with formidable competition. The chief practitioner of idleness in the essay is Mr. Sober, a man who fills "the day with petty business . . . [and has] always something in hand which may raise curiosity, but not solicitude, and keep the mind in a state of action but not of labour." His "chief pleasure is conversation"; he is terrified at the prospect of solitude and seeks to fill his time with mechanical tinkering. "His daily amusement is chemistry. . . . He . . . sits and counts the drops as they come from his retort, and forgets that, while a drop is falling, a moment flies away." This is severe self-criticism but not, for Johnson, surprising.

The sketch of Gelaleddin in *Idler* 75 continues the pattern, but with significant alterations. Gelaleddin, a young native of Tauris, is described as "amiable in his manners and beautiful in his form, of boundless curiosity, incessant diligence, and irresistible genius, of quick apprehension and tenacious memory, accurate without narrowness, and eager for novelty without inconstancy." The intellectual attributes suggest Johnson, if the physical ones do not. Gelaleddin is offered a professorship at Bassora, but instead seeks wealth and power in Tauris, believing he can always fall back upon "academical obscurity." His expectations are systematically blighted. His father sees him as an additional financial burden. His eloquence impresses neither the poor nor his brothers and sisters, who are preoccupied with their own indigence. He engenders envy among those who frequent "places of publick resort," and receives no employment from the visiers. He finally returns to Bassora where he is treated as "a fugitive, who returned only because he could live in no other place. . . . "

Johnson has altered the grounds for self-criticism. Gelaleddin is a victim of naiveté, not idleness. He is ignorant of the point which Johnson makes at length in the *Journey*, the fact that immediate wants may be so pressing that there is little room left for learning and letters. Gelaleddin is apparently unaware of the tenuous, evanescent nature of worldly fame, the fact that greatness changes as the context which produced it changes. The mature Johnson continually treats these issues; Gelaleddin is learning the implicit lessons firsthand. What is striking in the self-portrait is the introduction of factors which mitigate the self-criticism. Gelaleddin is victimized by innocence, illusion, and ambition but he is also endowed with an imposing list of intellectual and moral strengths. Johnson's admission that he had his own situation in mind when composing the piece hardly suggests self-laceration. Moreover, Gelaleddin's failings are common to the rest of mankind, though his abilities are decidedly uncommon, and his suffering results as much from a world of poverty, envy, and fear, as it does a lack of experience or a culpable desire for "greatness." There is blame here, but praise as well; the balancing of both, in my judgment, constitutes the major characteristic of Johnson's self-portraits.

The best modern commentary on the *Prayers and Meditations* has directed attention to two important matters. The first is the extent to which one falsifies Johnson's work by reading it rapidly. The result is nearly always the sense that Johnson's resolutions and failure to fulfill his own expectations come as swiftly as one can read them. Johnson's psychological stability is called into question without proper basis, for Johnson's self-examinations and resolves were usually keyed to some liturgical event or date with strong personal associations: his birthday, the anniversary of the death of his wife, the beginning of an important project, and, of course, New Year's. Second, Johnson's

low assessment of his own achievements does not spring from a
lack of awareness of the importance or the difficulty of his
completed tasks, but rather from a realization of what he could
accomplish, should he determine to do so. He is thoroughly
aware of the talents which God has bestowed upon him as well
as the fact that much more is, accordingly, demanded of him.
Boswell realizes this, even if he does not use it properly:

The solemn text, "of him to whom much is given, much will be
required," seems to have been ever present to his mind, in a rigorous
sense, and to have made him dissatisfied with his labours and acts of
goodness, however comparatively great; so that the unavoidable
consciousness of his superiority was, in that respect, a cause of
disquiet. (*Life*, IV, 427)

Even George III could appeal to this principle and indicate the
responsibilities which attend ability:

Johnson said, he thought he had already done his part as a writer. "I
should have thought so too, (said the King,) if you had not written so
well." — Johnson observed to me, upon this, that "No man could have
paid a handsomer compliment; and it was fit for a King to pay. It was
decisive." (*Life*, II, 35)

Pride and humility are simultaneously generated by the parable
of the talents; in Johnson they represent complementary sides of
a complex human reality. All too often, particularly in the
nineteenth century, they have been separated. Stress fell upon
Johnson's devastating pride in public, social performances, his
abject humility in private, devotional contexts, and both the
pride and the humility were judged aberrational. On the one
hand there was the conversational titan, carving or bludgeoning
the opposition with cleverness and the sheer force of personality, on the other a cringing victim of religious excess,
scrupulous to a fault. The pride and humility cannot be
separated in this fashion; indeed they are mutually defining and
must be seen in tandem, a pattern which frequently appears in
Johnson's works.

Although I disagree with some of Lawrence Lipking's conclusions concerning Johnsonian self-portraiture I am in full
agreement with his attitude toward its use:

Johnson's writings teem with self-references, with efforts to be acquainted with himself, with moral analysis of his own psychological predicaments. . . . Many Johnsonians carry within them an anthology . . . from which they recreate, moment by moment, a version of Johnson's spiritual autobiography. Why has that anthology not been published? To some extent its absence constitutes the most puzzling omission in the canon of Johnsonian biography. . . . And how remarkable that not one of Johnson's biographers, so far as I can find, has chosen to focus on the moving Latin poem, full of self-doubt and self-analysis, that Johnson wrote upon revising his Dictionary, and gave the Greek title of "Know thyself"! Is it possible that what *Johnson* thought about Johnson counts for so very little?[4]

The poem to which Lipking quite properly refers was completed after the revision for the fourth edition of the Dictionary. Readers of *Idler* 31 will not be surprised by Johnson's sentiments, here quoted in Arthur Murphy's translation:

> My task perform'd, and all my labours o'er,
> For me what lot has Fortune now in store?
> The listless will succeeds, that worst disease,
> The rack of indolence, the sluggish ease.
> Care grows on care, and o'er my aching brain
> Black melancholy pours her morbid train.
> No kind relief, no lenitive at hand,
> I seek at midnight clubs, the social band;
> But midnight clubs, where wit with noise conspires,
> Where Comus revels, and where wine inspires,
> Delight no more; I seek my lonely bed,
> And call on sleep to sooth my languid head.
> . . . .
> Whate'er I plan, I feel my pow'rs confin'd
> By Fortune's frown and penury of mind.
> I boast no knowledge glean'd with toil and strife,
> That bright reward of a well-acted life.
> I view myself, while reason's feeble light
> Shoots a pale glimmer through the gloom of night,

---

4. Lawrence Lipking, "Art, Morals, Madness," pp. 18-19. In his recent edition of selected *Lives of the Poets*, John Wain calls this poem "perhaps the most poignant piece of self-revelation in all [Johnson's] works" (p. ix). The problem is partially solved by the general availability of crucial texts in Wain's new *Johnson on Johnson.*

> While passions, error, phantoms of the brain
> And vain opinions, fill the dark domain;
> A dreary void, where fears with grief combin'd
> Waste all within, and desolate the mind.
>   What then remains? Must I in slow decline
> To mute inglorious ease old age resign?
> Or, bold ambition kindling in my breast,
> Attempt some arduous task? Or, were it best
> Brooding o'er lexicons to pass the day,
> And in that labour drudge my life away?
>   (*Poems*, p. 274)

The very act of committing one's mental state to verse is an assertion, and in Johnson's case a powerful one. The indolence of which he writes would be trivial were it not for the magnitude of the task which he has accomplished. The laborious drudgery which he foresees as a possible way of life jostles with his lofty ambitions. The element of pride and self-confidence is most apparent in the poem when we consider the manner in which our response would be altered if Johnson were not its author. If the poem had been written by a hack or poetaster after the completion of a now forgotten work, we would consider it mannered, pretentious posturing. The success of the poem turns on the stature of its author.

In similar fashion Johnson may term his lexicographic task the work of "a harmless drudge," but in the final paragraph of the Dictionary's Preface he turns to autobiographical concerns and assumes a stance of near-heroic indifference, maintaining a fragile balance between arrogance and high nobility:

The *English Dictionary* was written with little assistance of the learned, and without any patronage of the great; not in the soft obscurities of retirement, or under the shelter of academick bowers, but amidst inconvenience and distraction, in sickness and in sorrow. It may repress the triumph of malignant criticism to observe, that if our language is not here fully displayed, I have only failed in an attempt which no human powers have hitherto completed. . . .

. . . I have protracted my work till most of those whom I wished to please have sunk into the grave, and success and miscarriage are empty sounds: I therefore dismiss it with frigid tranquillity, having little to fear or hope from censure or from praise.

Commenting on the work of the literary scholar in the *Preface to Shakespeare,* Johnson writes that "the subjects to be discussed by him are of very small importance; they involve neither property nor liberty; nor favour the interest of sect or party" (*Johnson on Shakespeare,* VII, 102). However, Johnson's pride complements his humility, for Pope's comments on "the dull duty of an editor" bring a swift rejoinder: "Conjectural criticism demands more than humanity possesses, and he that exercises it with most praise has very frequent need of indulgence. Let us now be told no more of the dull duty of an editor" (p. 95).

In *The Vision of Theodore* Johnson assumes the role of adviser and boldly counsels the youthful readers of Dodsley's *Preceptor*—in which the work appeared—concerning such weighty issues as the relation between Reason and Religion and the nature of human motivation. Yet when he, in the allegory, describes the "Maze of Indolence" which ends in the dominion of Melancholy, who finally consigns her prisoners to the cruel control of Despair, we sense an intense portrayal of personal religious experience which is highly self-critical. In the *Journey* Johnson assumes the role of Enlightenment empiricist, challenging Scottish credulity; at the same time he admits his own shortcomings, the opportunities he has missed and facts he has forgotten. He dictates to the Scots concerning the cultivation (in the broadest sense) of their lands and people but is able, simultaneously, to portray himself with humility and gentle humor:

Here I first mounted a little Highland steed; and if there had been many spectators, should have been somewhat ashamed of my figure in the march. The horses of the Islands, as of other barren countries, are very low: they are indeed musculous and strong, beyond what their size gives reason for expecting; but a bulky man upon one of their backs makes a very disproportionate appearance. (*Journey,* p. 121)

In the *Rambler* Johnson toys with the image of the eidolon which he has himself created. Mr. Rambler's fondness for gloom, wretchedness, and hard words is lamented by fictional correspondents. The humor turns on Johnson's awareness and exploitation of his carefully constructed shortcomings and perversities, a process roughly paralleling his parodying of his own "prejudices" in light conversation.[5] He jettisons Steele's paradigm of the social commentator and moral adviser as a man of near flawless virtue and offers his own alternative. In *Rambler* 155 he indicates that the giving of advice involves an implicit claim of superiority which generally proves unpalatable and, finally, inefficacious. As Shaftesbury put it, the free gift of advice takes from another and adds to ourself (*Characteristics*, I, 103). Some degree of superiority, on the other hand, would seem to be necessary, for, as Johnson writes in *Rambler* 14, "men would not more patiently submit to be taught, than commanded, by one known to have the same follies and weaknesses with themselves." The ideal would be an adviser who can serve as an example as well. Because the number of such individuals is miniscule, Steele and his legion of imitators generally constructed idealized eidolons who were largely separated from their creators. Johnson, on the other hand, has been attacked for blurring the author/eidolon line. In point of fact Johnson's practice suggests that of Montaigne rather than Addison and Steele. Although there are halfhearted attempts to separate Mr. Rambler from Johnson, they are actually very much alike. Johnson's eidolon combines pride and humility. He possesses authority but he is sufficiently fallen to alleviate any qualms concerning hypocrisy. His task is twofold. He must exhibit the humility which he recommends throughout the periodical as an alternative to vanity and vain desire, yet maintain a sufficient degree of self-assurance to bring his points home without dissipating them in a flood of modesty and timidity. This explains, I think, much of the running dialogue with the audience in which Mr. Rambler informs them of his awareness of his unpopularity but his determination to push on and conduct matters in his own way. He admits that he lacks certain strengths and must capitalize on those he does possess. He confesses shortcomings but maintains his courage. He displays warmth but also independence, insecurity (to an extent) but also confidence. The same figure who humbly writes that he has "never been much a favourite of the publick" (no. 208), can

5. See A. T. Elder, "Irony and Humour in the *Rambler*."

also announce that "the men who can be charged with fewest failings, either with respect to abilities or virtue, are generally most ready to allow them. . . . " (no. 31).

The praise/blame, pride/humility pattern may appear in secular contexts but its basis, for Johnson, is religious. Joseph Towers summarizes the pattern precisely:

When the great intellectual powers that Dr. Johnson possessed are considered, and the rapidity with which he finished his compositions, when he could prevail on himself to sit down to write, little doubt can be entertained, but that he might have produced much more than he did; and it was probably this consciousness that occasioned his frequent self-reproaches.[6]

John Wain writes that "Johnson's sense of his own intellectual and spiritual power was a torture to him. For, if much had been given to him, correspondingly much would be asked. The parable of the steward who let his talent lie unused . . , was terrible to him" (*Samuel Johnson*, p. 55; cf. pp. 286, 369). On Johnson's completion of tasks Hawkins comments that

this remission of his labour, which seemed to be no more than nature herself called for, Johnson, in those severe audits to which it was his practice to summon himself, would frequently condemn, styling it a waste of his time, and a misapplication of the talents with which he was gratefully conscious that God had endowed him. (Hawkins, *Life*, pp. 350-51)

Haller notes the importance of the parable for the Puritans: "No part of the Puritan code was more weighted with practical significance than this" (*The Rise of Puritanism*, p. 124). However, Johnson can be far more severe than the Puritans. Milton may be correct in his nineteenth sonnet when he writes that "God doth not need / Either man's work or his own gifts" but Johnson would argue that He still demands them and is far less comfortable than Milton with the notion of standing and waiting. In this general context at least, Wain's judgment that Milton "was in some ways less Puritan than Johnson" (*Johnson as Critic*, p. 31) is accurate.

6. O M Brack, Jr., and Robert E. Kelley, eds., *The Early Biographies of Samuel Johnson*, p. 219.

The parable of the talents is closely linked with a double vision of man which is profoundly Christian, the notion that our misery and our greatness are near allied. Our accomplishments remind us of our heavenly connections, our failures of our earthly ones. In a sense our pride and humility are not only mutually defining but inseparable. John Dunne treats this pattern in the works of Pascal, Luther, and Erasmus (*A Search for God in Time and Memory*, p. 87), but the thesis statement is most often drawn from Pascal:

Christianity is strange. It bids man recognize that he is vile, yea, abominable, and it bids him try to be like God. Without that counterpoise, such an uplift would render him horribly vain, or the humiliation would render him terribly abject.

Christianity then teaches men these twin truths together: that there is a God whom men can reach, and that there is a corruption in their nature which renders them unworthy of Him. Knowledge of both these points is equally important for man; and it is equally dangerous for man to know God without knowing his own misery, and to know his misery without knowing the Redeemer who can cure it. Knowledge of one alone causes either the pride of philosophers who have known God but not their misery, or the despair of atheists who know their misery but not their Redeemer.[7]

The eighteenth century would be particularly aware of this part of Pascal's thought, for the fragmentary version of the *Pensées* which would be in most common use, Kennet's, organizes Pascal's thoughts in a series of chapters, several of which are germane to the issue of man's double nature:

III: The true Religion proved by the Contrarieties which are discoverable in Man, and by the Doctrine of Original Sin.
XXI: The strange Contrarieties discoverable in Human Nature, with regard to Truth and Happiness, and many other Things.
XXIII: The Greatness of Man.
XXIV: The Vanity of Man.

7. *Pascal's Pensées*, pp. 189, 7. John Barker (*Strange Contrarieties*) points out Pascal's literary impact and the fact that comments such as this were cited in periodical essays and elsewhere. "All the evidence suggests that the general theme in the *Pensées* to which men with literary interests most responded was the analysis by . . . Pascal of man's paradoxical nature" (p. 113).

Johnson's regard for Pascal is well known;[8] he shares the view of human nature which Pascal articulates and realizes that the simultaneous sense of power and impotence, of pride and humility, is intensified in the individual whose gifts are most uncommon. There is an unsettling dynamism built into the Christian life. The more one does the more he realizes how much is left undone. The more one aspires to goodness the more he is conscious of weakness. As Johnson tells Boswell, "The better a man is, the more afraid he is of death, having a clearer view of infinite purity" (Life, III, 154). Such a Christian can never aspire to rest or contentment within the confines of this world and is doomed to the restlessness of which Augustine writes, a restlessness of crucial thematic importance in Johnson's work, particularly in Rasselas.

The parable of the talents is an essential part of a vision of history as well as a vision of human nature. The relation between our abilities and accomplishments suggests our simultaneous grandeur and depravity. Both are epitomized in the Incarnation. Man is important enough for God to send His only Son into our midst; man is so pitiful that nothing short of the coming of the Son of God can save him. Within the Christian vision, the historical event of the Incarnation is intimately bound up with notions of human nature. John Dunne writes that "the story of God among men as a man, persuading and dissuading yet not compelling, is perhaps our best clue to what God is and what man is" (The Way of All the Earth, p. 194). In the dramatic, right-angled Christian vision of history, treated so well by Professor Abrams in Natural Supernaturalism, the Incarnation is a staggering event. Jung comments:

The Christian's ordinary conception of God is of an omnipotent, omniscient, and all-merciful Father and Creator of the world. If this God wishes to become man, an incredible kenosis (emptying) is required of Him, in order to reduce His totality to the infinitesimal

---

8. With Boswell the case is a bit more difficult. Barker (p. 164) comments that a GM essay on Pascal, possibly by Boswell, "marks the high point of later eighteenth-century English suspicion, contempt, and ridicule." In other contexts, of course, Boswell praises Pascal. For a discussion of the GM piece see Pottle, The Literary Career of James Boswell, Esq., pp. 231-32.

human scale. Even then it is hard to see why the human frame is not shattered by the incarnation. . . . The Christian God-image cannot become incarnate in empirical man without contradictions. . . . (*Memories, Dreams, Reflections*, p. 337)

Man, who would imitate Christ, that is, divinity, finds Christ becoming man. Dunne writes that

When we make humanity our aim . . . and enter thereby into a sympathetic understanding of the passion of Christ, we discover that the fulfilled or hardened or detached being that we had imagined to be divine on the basis of our own desire to be God is not the genuine God, but the genuine God is the one who loses himself as God in order that man may be born. (*A Search for God in Time and Memory*, p. 23)

To aspire to divinity is to aspire to full humanity, as Blake—for whom the parable of the talents was also of compelling importance—tells us again and again. "Therefore God becomes as we are, that we may be as he is" (*THERE is NO Natural Religion*, b).

What is particularly striking in all this is the manner in which Johnsonian practice accommodates a crucial portion of eighteenth-century theory. A life-writer's work must be of benefit to his reader, the exemplary value of the work partly turning on the extent to which the biographical subject's experience can be generalized. Despite all of the particular details and contexts of Johnsonian self-portraiture, the way to a larger context is always before us, and in a sense the context is the most important of all, the mutually defining relation of man to God. Jung writes that "although we human beings have our own personal life, we are yet in large measure the representatives, the victims and promoters of a collective spirit whose years are counted in centuries" (*Memories, Dreams, Reflections*, p. 91) and Goethe argues that "every one must form himself as a particular being, seeking, however, to attain that general idea of which all mankind are constituents" (Eckermann, *Words of Goethe*, p. 115).

Each human life recapitulates common human experience. The result for life-writing very often is an element of structural predictability so that even the vivid, particularized account of which Johnson is capable has certain affinities with forms as stylized as saints' lives, criminal biographies, and Puritan autobiographies. In Johnson's self-portraits we immediately confront a larger pattern, and the differences between Johnson and Boswell in this regard are important. The relationships which interest Boswell are those of man to land, family, class, and position. Boswell stresses these patterns in Johnson, excessively in my judgment, while failing to come to terms with the pattern which, for Johnson, is of paramount importance, the relation of man to God. Boswell suffers because he perceives life as mystery rather than as paradox. He seeks to understand, while Johnson seeks to cope. The problem for Johnson is not one of understanding, but of dealing with a situation which is intelligible but which, at the outset, removes the possibility of rest and contentment. Thus Johnson is impatient with Boswellian melancholy, partly because Boswell is self-indulgent with it, but chiefly because it is of a lower order than his own.

I would not argue that the pride and humility which result from Johnson's intense awareness of the parable of the talents are sufficient unto themselves as a biographer's "image," that is, more would be necessary if one were writing Johnson's life. This pattern is a very important one and explains a great deal but it is, obviously, a very general pattern. The "image" which emerges from modern scholarship might be something like this:

Samuel Johnson. Englishman from Staffordshire, of middle class parentage, respectable but poor. He moves from trying familial and financial positions to success as a professional writer. Essentially, he is a moralist and hortatory psychologist, an energetic and incisive scholar. He is one of the few post-Renaissance prose writers who writes in a recognizable style; he is an accomplished poet, one whose verse has still not received the attention it deserves. He is perhaps the greatest literary critic who has ever lived but one who is, in the best sense of the word, unsystematic. He gives his name to his age but he is not always of that age. He dislikes much eighteenth-century literature and is fundamentally at odds with the spirit and practice of satire. He lambasts such brahmins as Pope, Swift, and Gray and prefers biography at a time when it is seldom written with great effectiveness. He is a rebellious conservative who espouses Tory and High Church norms in an age of Whigs and skeptics; his allegiance, however, is always to the eternal. His norms are never strictly partisan. He is willing to attack anyone when Christian norms are violated. He is in tune with all of the fundamental tenets of the Enlightenment except for its libertinism and antireligious skepticism. For all of his uniqueness, to himself he is everyman. His own image for himself, a mixture of pride and humility, turns on the importance of the parable of the talents within the Christian vision and it is the general nature of this pattern which seizes his attention. He is both a human being and a quasi-fictional character in a great book. Largely because of that book, he is a crucial part of Western consciousness, but not always for the right reasons. His works justify that position, but their role—chiefly because of Boswell and the tradition he initiates—has all too often been a subservient one.

A brief sketch such as this does not begin to touch on the varied aspects of Johnson's experience. I include it only to highlight some of the interests of Johnson's modern students and indicate, by implication, a part of the disparity between our Johnson and Boswell's. It could be argued that "images" of Johnson may be traced in the *Life*, "images" which I have not treated. In a sense that is true. There are repeating references to Johnson which follow certain patterns, for example, Johnson as modern Hercules or Socrates, but such images usually serve to elucidate certain facets of Johnson's personality as Boswell perceives them. For an overarching, sophisticated image based on an awareness of the available material, an image which is used systematically to organize materials for the reader, one looks, in my judgment, in vain.

Boswell's vision of Johnson's life consists, essentially, of a series of images: Johnson in conversation, Johnson in encounters, Johnson in "scenes." The pattern suggests the pictorialist tradition of which Jean Hagstrum writes (*The Sister Arts,* esp. pp. 181, 256), a tradition which in poetry generates structures which suggest picture galleries. Such poetry, "in which we move from scene to scene, tableau to tableau" is a kind of "pageant with interpretative comment." A poem (or biography) like this "is a *display* of personages whose mental and physical measure is being taken and who reveal their character in what they are seen to be and heard to say" (p. 181).

In the London Journal Boswell recounts some comments made by Dempster:

He considered the mind of man like a room, which is either made agreeable or the reverse by the pictures with which it is adorned. External circumstances are nothing to the purpose. Our great point is to have pleasing pictures in the inside. . . . The great art is to have an agreeable collection and to preserve them well. (p. 203)

Boswell comments, "This is really an ingenious and lively fancy. . . . [As a man] grows up, he gets some substantial pieces which he always preserves, although he may alter his smaller paintings in a moment" (pp. 203-4). This, it seems to me, is an excellent introduction to the manner in which Boswell shapes experience and there is no question that many of his "substantial pieces" were to be pictures of Johnson. As we read such works as Johnson's "Annals" we find that *his* sense of experience is fluid and varied. Thousands of details, each rich with associations, combine in his memory and constitute his identity. From the man-midwife Hector's "Here is a brave boy!" to his final "GOD bless you, my dear!" the elements in Johnson's memory would lead in one of two directions: either to a multivolumed autobiography, encyclopedic in scope and nearly so in length, or to a single image which would depict Johnson's striving to utilize his talents and imitate his Lord, a picture like Blake's of Albion standing with outstretched arms before the crucified Christ. Boswell's memories are beautifully, poignantly, and appropriately portrayed as a series of scenes in a play or pictures in a gallery, few in number but each of vast importance; Johnson's are not.

CHAPTER VI

The Uses of the *Life*

*I have a peculiar treasure which my assiduity has secured—A
great number of his Conversations taken down exactly—scenes
Which were highly delightfull at the time and will forever afford
instruction and entertainment. How dismal a Blank dos his
departure make! I stretch after him with enthusiastick eagerness.
I cannot doubt that he is exalted to immortal felicity. (Corr—
Club, p. 176)*

F. L. Lucas complains that critics argue over the "pleasure-
value" of literature (a futile activity), while neglecting
its "influence-value." Literature's influence and consequences
can and should be discussed, but here critics are often "ob-
stinately silent" (*Literature and Psychology*, p. 216). Lucas'
complaint has never been totally applicable in the case of
Boswell, for the consequences of his work—whether good or
ill—have always been of some importance. Boswell's popular
success is demonstrable and it results, to some extent, from
considerable strengths. However, the extent of Boswell's influence has also resulted in a realization of his shortcomings. In a
sense he has proven to be his own worst literary enemy. His
success has singled him out among biographers but at the same
time it has isolated him and exposed him to criticism. The *Life* is
often judged a model biography but models must meet
requirements that are particularly stringent. Ideal or absolute
norms are shown to be unreasonable when they are tested
against discrete, model texts. In the process, however, the

models' weaknesses (in terms of absolute standards) are illuminated. The importance of the *Life* has generated increased interest in its weaknesses and because of his eminence Boswell is sometimes dealt with more harshly than biographers of a second order such as Walton.

A parallel situation exists with Boswell's treatment of his biographical subject. For Boswell, Johnson's importance is inestimable. His value as an exemplum is enormous; all possible details of his life must be cherished and preserved. However, as we begin to accept Boswell's point of view, perhaps even to share his reverence for Johnson, we become harsher with Johnson's biographer. We wish to know much more than Boswell tells us; we are impatient with any sign on Boswell's part of indolence or inaccuracy, and vexed by any imprecision in Boswell's handling of Johnson's personality and thought. Boswell is at pains to convince us of Johnson's greatness but the result of his efforts is a more rigorous examination of his treatment of his biographical subject.

Earlier we discussed the question of "artifice" and "reality" within the *Life* and the manner in which these may be subtly interconnected or confused. A similar situation occurs in the response of readers to the semifictive dimensions of the *Life.* In Boswell's biography of Johnson a real individual is portrayed. The portrayal, however, is such that Boswell's protagonist takes on many of the trappings of a fictional character. The problem in this situation is a normative one: is the exemplary value of a historical personage enhanced or diminished by the introduction of techniques associated with fiction? To phrase the question in different fashion, is the exemplary value of a biographical subject directly proportional to his *humanity?* The question is a difficult one and I shall not pretend to "solve" it. I think, however, that a realization of the problem's existence is important if one is to "use" the *Life* properly.

It is obvious that fictional characters may function as exempla. It is clear, for example, that hagiography often effaces any line separating history from fiction and the purpose of hagiography is, among other things, to influence through example. Even in the most "objective" biography, literary techniques and devices are unavoidable. Each biography will, to some extent, fictionalize its subject. The purely *human,* historically "accurate" subject, free of all shaping and manipulation, is impossible. What should concern us is excessive or improper manipulation. If, for example, Johnson is consistently portrayed in certain contexts to the exclusion of others or if his private devotional writings are slanted by careful "editing," the *Life's* exemplary value is diminished. We may be moved by or impressed with Boswell's protagonist but this figure is not necessarily Samuel Johnson. He may be "real" in the sense that he is "rounded" or "fully realized" but he is not "real" historically.

The problem of the *Life* in this regard lies in the fact that Boswell's Johnson is sometimes "real" in one sense but not always in the other and to challenge Boswell is a jarring and disruptive (albeit necessary) activity. In correcting the *Life* as history we fracture certain literary relationships and associations. It is discomforting to be told that memorable scenes and passages involve gross falsification. Thus, those who quite properly challenge Boswell are often cast in the role of annoying revisionists: carpers and detractors who overlook Boswell's strengths in their passion for disclosing his weaknesses. This overreaction is largely generated by shattered literary illusions. Few are troubled when they are told that a historical work is dated or now shown to be inaccurate. To be told, however, that an "inspired" lyric is a pastiche or that a highly praised novel has been read with no awareness of the fact that chapters were inadvertently transposed, is unsettling indeed. The conflict is between Boswell's artistic achievement and his accuracy and objectivity, and it should be noted that his claims of perfect authenticity have not aided his defense.

The defensiveness of Boswell's students is to be expected, for more is at stake than the quality of a particular eighteenth-century book. Frye comments that "those who have most effectively changed the modern world . . . are those who have changed the general pattern of our mythology" (*The Stubborn Structure,* p. 32). Frye is here thinking of Rousseau, Marx, and Freud, but the statement may also, with certain qualifications, be applied to Boswell. He may not have changed the modern world but he has most definitely altered the manner in which we think. Macaulay's judgment, that Boswell's scenes and characters are permanent fixtures in our consciousness, is still an accurate one. On the title page of the *Life* Boswell promises, among other things, an account of a period, and for many the *Life* still *is*, in large measure, that period. The importance of the chief figure in that period has never been greater. Lockhart realized Johnson's exemplary value from the beginning and argued that

in spite of innumerable oddities, and of many laughable and some few condemnable weaknesses, when we desire to call up the notion of a human being thoroughly, as far as our fallen clay admits the predication of such qualities, good and wise; in the whole of his mind lofty, of his temper generous, in the midst of misery incapable of *shabbiness*, "every inch a *man*,"—the name of Samuel Johnson springs to every lip. (*Biography as an Art*, p. 76)

Johnson himself was concerned with the manner in which all phases of human endeavor—both highbrow and popular—affect the processes of human thought. (He is far less narrow in this regard than most literary scholars.) Were he here now he would be fascinated with the extent to which his thought has permeated not only highbrow but also popular culture. He is quoted (or misquoted) on television programs (often by other formidable talkers such as Perry Mason). One greeting card company quotes his remark on keeping friendships in repair as part of its advertising. (Very recently I encountered an advertisement for a food market which quoted Johnson on the notion of curiosity as a primary characteristic of a vigorous intellect. The ad encouraged curiosity, surprise, and responsiveness and then invited potential patrons to inspect the market's produce.) Johnson is even the subject of fictional detective stories and his Hebridean tour has recently spawned an interesting cookbook with interspersed Rowlandson caricatures. Nearly all of this sort of thing is traceable to Boswell, just as the continuing flow of popular biographies of Johnson is stimulated by the *Life*, the primary source for most popular biographers.

To challenge Boswell is, to a great extent, to challenge the way we think, and such challenges involve considerable risk, for revisionist approaches to Boswell do not always offer tidy alternatives. Students are informed that Boswell's presentation of a facet of Johnson's thought is inaccurate; they are then encouraged to familiarize themselves with contemporary scholarship, read volumes of Johnson's works, scattered individual pieces (often difficult of access and in unfamiliar genres), and develop an alternative to Boswell. Instead of an amusing caricature or a larger-than-life portrait, they are often left with a complex pattern of thought and behavior and a series of cautious qualifications and distinctions. The implicit assumption here is that *human* beings have more exemplary value than semifictive ones and that the "real" Johnson will ultimately prove far more satisfying than the Johnson which Boswell offers. The real Johnson, however, is neither as readily available nor as easy to deal with as Boswell's.

What Boswell *does* offer is a wealth of material, much of it unavailable elsewhere. In the epigraph quoted above Boswell points to his treasure: Johnson's conversations and the scenes in which they occur. Here Boswell's contribution is of considerable value. Boswell also, however, prides himself on the inclusion of Johnson's private correspondence:

I am absolutely certain that *my* mode of Biography which gives not only a *History* of Johnson's *visible* progress through the World, and of his Publications, but a *View* of his mind, in his Letters, and Conversations is the most perfect that can be conceived, and will be *more* of a *Life* than any Work that has ever yet appeared. (*Corr—Life*, p. 267)

The question of the correspondence is complex. The inclusion of the letters was striking and, in some quarters, shocking. Their usefulness for us on the other hand is, in a sense, minimal, for Boswell prints only a portion (perhaps one-fifth) of Johnson's correspondence. As a resource Boswell is totally superseded by Chapman. Nearly all of Boswell's "scholarly" activity—his inclusion of some Johnsonian verse, the French tour diary, variants in the *Lives of the Poets*, for example—have been or will be superseded, and in some cases (for example his unreliable account of the prose canon) he has caused as many problems as he has solved. In this sort of area Johnson scholars will turn elsewhere for help, partly because of Boswell's influence. Boswell's demonstration of Johnson's importance has partly led to our realization of Boswell's inadequacy. Hence Donald Greene's suggestion:

Would it not be better to break up [the *Life*] into the component parts which Boswell so loosely and perfunctorily strung together—to extract the parts deriving from the journal and publish them separately as *Boswell's Conversations with Johnson,* following the example of Eckermann? Does not whatever artistry Boswell contributed to the *Life* consist in them alone, and would not that artistry be enhanced by such a procedure? (" 'Tis A Pretty Book, Mr. Boswell, But—," p. 7)

As Greene points out, Postgate did this sort of thing in 1930 with a certain amount of success; his collection has been reprinted on several occasions. The suggestion is not without merit. After all, the *Life* continually appears in abridged versions and though a distaste for abridgement, on principle, is in some ways admirable, I suspect that the abridging of Boswell meets with a far different reaction than the abridging of other types of works. Pottle's distinction between Boswell's imaginative, as opposed to inventive power ("The Life of Boswell," p. 449) is a useful one. ("In *imaginative* power Boswell is the peer of Scott and Dickens, in *inventive* power he is nowhere in comparison with them.") We are most upset by the tampering with "inventive" literature. Boswell's inventions often should be deleted; his "imaginative" materials are almost always retained when the *Life* is abridged.

The problem of implementing such a procedure turns on the relation between the *Life's* scenes and its larger structures. Certain "dead space," for example, is crucial to the meeting-with-Wilkes scene; to be effective, the scene must be presented in toto. However, it is fair to ask whether or not the "dead space" in other parts of the *Life* also needs to be retained. The best study of this issue, in my judgment, is Paul Alkon's "Boswellian Time." Alkon argues, very plausibly, that Boswell is perturbed by the disparity between Johnson's experience and the amount of attention it receives in Mrs. Piozzi's *Anecdotes.* "Boswell implies that perfect, or even merely adequate, authenticity can scarcely exist in a genre where there is a temporal disproportion as great as the difference between twenty years [of experience] and two hours [of reading time]" (p. 241). Boswell must somehow simulate the sense of seventy-five years' experience without producing a Shandean monstrosity. He is heartened by the amount of dead space in real life, a point made by Johnson in *Rambler* 8, and relies on structural devices (some with thematic dimensions) to create the illusion in the reader's mind of a vast accumulation of experience over an extended period of time. One way he accomplishes this is by spending so much time on the later years. "By devoting more and more pages to less and less real time as lived by Johnson, . . . Boswell slows the book's psychological tempo and compels the reader's inner clock to tick ever more slowly" (pp. 247-48). The liberal sprinkling of dates conveys a certain sense of temporal flow and the recurrence of certain types of scenes "decelerate[s] the sense of temporal motion" (p. 249). Moreover, the portrayal of character is nonprogressive. The child-as-father-of-the-man theoretical base generates a rhetoric of accumulation rather than progression and the mixing of time levels ("Today Johnson said . . . which reminds me of what he once told Hector . . . which suggests a comment in his *Life of Pope* . . . "), of which Passler writes at length, also slows the *Life's* tempo.

This, it seems to me, is quite cogent, and the inclusion of letters, notes, and gimcrackery like Johnson's legal opinions or "*Various Readings in the Life of* Blackmore" does slow the book's tempo. These materials do have an effect on the book and they may well be a matter of conscious structural design. However, the fact that many of Boswell's materials serve a function does not entirely justify the utter dullness of many of them. Boswell's practices may be explained but the explanation may not be suitable compensation for his readers.

Similarly, Boswell's practices may be based on acceptable literary principles but questionable philosophic ones. His view of personality and identity, for example, is far less compelling than Hume's. It may square with a facet of Johnsonian theory but it does not square, consistently, with Johnsonian practice. If the notion of a fixed personality does not wash, Boswell's procedure—illustrating that personality through carefully selected specimens—may be called into question. Even admitting the viability of Boswell's approach, one must also question the accuracy and sophistication of *Boswell's* sense of Johnson's personality.

It is also fair to point out that the fixed personality/rhetoric of accumulation pattern is not Boswell's sole option. He could slow the book's tempo in other ways, for example, through a greater density of prose texture or by a careful subdividing of material. It is easy to accept Charles Burney's description of the *Life* as "uncommonly alluring" (*Corr—Club*, p. 343); to see it as the greatest biography which we have is quite another matter, for Boswell's procedures are open to question on many fronts. Burke's description of the *Life* as "the Most entertaining Book he had ever read" (*Corr—Life*, p. 425) should be taken quite seriously but we should not overlook Burke's comment that "many particulars there related might as well have been omitted" (*Corr—Life*, p. 431). Geoffrey Scott says of the *Life* that it is "the masterpiece which, more than most great books, has added to the stock of happiness" (*PP*, VI, 290). That, it seems to me, is not only accurate but an appropriate use of a frequently neglected Johnsonian principle. However, to say that it is a great book should not be equated with the claim that it is a great biography.

An obvious point, but one which should always be made on Boswell's behalf, concerns his choice of subject. He contemplated lives of such figures as Hume, Walton, Dick, Oglethorpe, Kames, and Pringle; he wrote a life of Johnson, and it is hard to imagine a figure whose experience was more congenial to Boswell's method. Not only is that experience of vast intrinsic worth; it is precisely commensurate with Boswell's abilities. Nor is it just to argue that the material wrote itself, that one could hardly fail in writing the life of such a man as Johnson, for many have demonstrated the ease with which one could fail in such an undertaking. Early in his life Boswell realized both his strengths and limitations. In 1762 he writes:

I told . . . [Lord Kames] that I should like much to be distinguished . . . [as an author], that I was sure that I had genius, and was not deficient in easiness of expression; but was at a loss for something to say, and, when I set myself seriously to think of writing, that I wanted a Subject. (*PP*, I, 101)

All his life he sought subjects suitable to his abilities and his most important decision in this regard was unerring.

The generic nature of the *Life* must be treated with greater precision. It is useful in this regard to begin with Flexner's observation that the biographer must appear in his book. The biographer's evidence will, perforce, be used with a degree of subjectivism so it is important that the audience become acquainted with the user, for "when an author keeps himself always in the background, we may only discover his prejudices by making a new study of the source material" (*Biography as an Art*, p. 179). In his work Boswell is not, like Eckermann, for example, a shadowy figure. He is in many ways at center stage. This may generate serious problems but only when we mistake the nature of the work with which we are dealing and treat it as "great biography." As F. L. Lucas argues, "The Life of Johnson is really only an outwork of a far huger Life of Boswell"; "his biography is, in some sense, a by-product of an immense autobiography" (*The Search for Good Sense*, pp. 261, 266). What is remarkable is Boswell's ability to keep his own concerns in relative, but not complete abeyance, for his self-absorption is nearly complete:

Boswell was talking away one evening in St. James's Park with much vanity. Said his friend Temple, "We have heard of many kinds of hobby-horses, but, Boswell, you ride upon yourself." (*Boswelliana*, p. 208)

For the Romantics, building upon eighteenth-century epistemology, the subjectivity at work in life-writing or historiography is central. "Authenticity," as Croker pointed out, turns on point of view as much as on hard facts. Francis Hart writes:

Such stress on the personality of the memoirist reflects the essence of Romantic thought—the assumption that experience is dominated by the subjectivity at its center, that the subject "knows" its object by knowing itself in the object, and that therefore the historian-biographer's knowledge is a mode of his personal experience. In the post-Malahide era it has been easy enough to discover that Boswell's Johnson is an inseparable part of Boswell's Boswell. ("Boswell and the Romantics," p. 61)

The problem in the case of Boswell lies in the fact that his subjectivism is so thoroughgoing:

Boswell, who had a good deal of whim, used not only to form wild projects in his imagination, but would sometimes reduce them to practice. In his calm hours he said with great good humour, "There have been many people who built castles in the air, but I believe I am the first that ever attempted to live in them." (*Boswelliana*, p. 225)

What concerns me are Boswell's attempts to make Johnson a fellow tenant. Lacking the ability to "Be Johnson," according to his own Journal dictates, he sometimes does, perhaps unconsciously, what *is* possible. He makes Johnson Boswell, and invests him with a nearly Catholic religious bent and an exaggerated Tory political posture, both of which falsify crucial aspects of Johnson's thought. Johnson is assiduously queried on matters which are really of greater importance to Boswell than to Johnson. His views of titles and traditions are played up; certain areas of his erudition are played down. He is visualized in social settings in social London. When, however, Boswell maintains a distance between himself and Johnson there is also the possibility of falsification, for the separation may involve a certain dehumanization. I think, for example, that Waingrow's description of Boswell's Johnson is a very good one. For Boswell, Johnson is something "steady, and steadying, of which Boswell stood in awesome contemplation." Thus,

the writing of the *Life* was more than memorial therapy, the patient ministering to himself; the hypochondriac turned artist steadied his own doctor and consoled *us* with the contemplation of something at least comparatively great. (*Corr—Life*, p. 1).

In the process, however, Boswell must play down such things as Johnson's flexibility and his intellectual growth. He may be transformed into a monument rather than a man. This may be "Boswell's Johnson" but it cannot wholly be ours. Johnson may well be, as Waingrow writes, "the apotheosis of sanity" (p. 1) but that sanity which we prize results from a constancy that is not *settled* but rather one that is based upon the most important kinds of agitation, concern, and doubt. Boswell knows of this agitation, of course, but much prefers the self-assured, composed, solid figure surrounded by a world of perplexity and change, a near-heroic alternative to much that is wrong in the world and much that is wrong in Boswell himself.

Boswell's *Life of Johnson* has been misused in various ways. The problem is not exclusively traceable to Boswell himself, but he is responsible for a large share of it. The claims of accuracy and authenticity, of assiduity and near perfection, have been accepted by many and the book praised as great biography. It has then been used as an entrée into Johnson's thought and personality, often as a substitute for the thought and personality which are available in Johnson's works. The biographer has replaced the biographical subject and in some quarters the biographer's presentation of the biographical subject's age has been accepted as an epitome or even as a panoramic view of that age. A "popular tradition" of Johnson—described so well by Professor Bronson—has flourished independently of serious scholarship and made communication of new insights and new learning unnecessarily difficult. Johnson has been valued primarily as a talker, necessitating a rediscovery of his works. In the twentieth century the discovery of the Boswell papers sometimes evoked the suggestion that Boswell was in fact a more important figure than Johnson. In the face of such silliness, a counter movement pointing up Boswell's limitations, shortcomings, and offenses was both predictable and salutary. It is now proper to inquire concerning the proper uses of the *Life*.

Certain things are obvious and I shall not belabor them. Earlier uses of the *Life* are of considerable interest to the student of literary and aesthetic history. The importance of the book for the Romantics, for example, is a matter which consistently merits attention. For the "Scottish Enlightenment," it seems to me, the book's uses are peripheral. The *Tour*, Johnson's *Journey*, and certain volumes of Boswell's Journal—with his political, social, and journalistic activities—are far more important here. Both the theory and practice of later biography are, in a sense, unintelligible without a consideration of the *Life* and it will continue to receive attention in this context. The issue which chiefly concerns me is the use of the *Life* by the student of Johnson. For such a student the book is a difficult one. He must constantly guard against Boswellian falsification of Johnson. To do this requires an ongoing skepticism, a judicious examination of the material as Boswell presents it. On nearly every page, suspicions and reservations lead to queries and qualifications. The result is that it is difficult to block these matters out and surrender oneself to Boswell; the pleasure of reading the *Life* is accordingly diminished. Nevertheless, Boswell is so adept and the popular traditions concerning Johnson so strong, that even the skeptical reader sometimes has difficulty remembering the most obvious matters.

For example, it is clear that Boswell was far less important to Johnson than the *Life* might suggest. He was important, to be sure, but so were Langton, Beauclerk, Burke, Reynolds, Goldsmith, Banks, Hector, Cave, James, and all the rest. Boswell's impact on Johnson is nothing compared to Johnson's impact on Boswell. Thus, when John Wain gives Boswell very short shrift in his biography of Johnson we realize that he is correct. Still, and this is my point, there is a touch of surprise, perhaps even shock, at Wain's procedure. To give a further example, we can demonstrate the fact that one should not be surprised by the fact that Boswell was not mentioned in Johnson's will, but still the matter continues to surprise us.

In reading the *Life* we must continually "correct for" Boswell if we are to be fair to Johnson, and the result is that we are unfair to Boswell's art. The alternative is no more appealing: the surrendering to Boswell's art with the subsequent falsification of Johnson. The best corrective, it seems to me, is to approach

Boswell from a different direction, to come to the *Life* from the Journal and private papers, to see the *Life* as essentially a book about Boswell, a portion of his autobiography. Boswell defines himself in relation to individuals, and his interaction with Johnson is more instructive than any other aspect of Boswell's life. In the case of Johnson the *Life* teaches us many things but the primary one is the effect that Johnson had on a particular individual, an individual who was not only quite different, in many ways, from Johnson but from many others as well. When the *Life* is viewed as biography the tendency is to circumscribe Johnson within the limits of Boswell's book. On the other hand, when the *Life* is properly viewed—as autobiography—we receive a glimpse of how great Johnson truly was by examining in detail his impact on a single individual. In the past, the small portion of Johnson's experience which Boswell's pages contain has led to great admiration for Boswell's biographical subject. The realization of Boswell's limitations should, properly, lead to far greater admiration.

When the events of the *Life* are set against the facts of Johnson's life and work (as these can be discerned) the result, very often, is the necessity for qualification and correction. On the other hand, when the events are set against the patterns of Boswell's life and the background provided by the Journal and private papers, the events are illuminated. One key example may suffice. B. L. Reid ("Johnson's Life of Boswell," pp. 556-57), like many others, has called attention to the masterful scene in which Johnson accompanies Boswell to Harwich for Boswell's departure for Holland (*Life,* I, 472). The event was of great importance for Boswell. He retained the receipt for his passage all his life (*PP,* I, 154). The event is anticipated pages before the departure itself:

After we had again talked of my setting out for Holland, he said "I must see thee out of England: I will accompany you to Harwich." I could not find words to express what I felt upon this unexpected and very great mark of his affectionate regard. (I, 462-63)

To leave Johnson, London, and all that they represent for Boswell is an unpleasant prospect. What is worse is that he leaves Johnson and London for Holland. The oppressiveness of Holland, coupled with Boswell's study of the law and resolve to remain continent will, in combination, nearly prove too much for him. What awaits him, in short, is gloom. He will not, however, be denied his final taste of all that is dear. The monarch of intellectual London is to see him off and several days earlier to do him "the honour to pass a part of the morning with [him] at [his, i.e., Boswell's] Chambers" (I, 463). During this brief period before the departure Johnson abounds in bon mots. Some of the most frequently quoted passages in the *Life* are from these few pages:

"Sir, a woman's preaching is like. . . . " (I, 463)

"I look upon it, that he who does not mind his belly will hardly mind any thing else." (I, 467)

"This was a good dinner enough, to be sure; but it was not a dinner to *ask* a man to." (I, 470)

A moth having fluttered round the candle, and burnt itself. . . . "That creature was its own tormentor, and I believe its name was BOSWELL." (I, 470)

"Don't, Sir, accustom yourself to use big words for little matters." (I, 471)

These pages also include the "refutation" of Berkeley scene and the more representative scene on the Harwich stage coach in which Johnson addresses a stranger, "a fat elderly gentlewoman" concerned with rearing her children and guarding against idleness: "JOHNSON. 'I wish, Madam, you would educate me too; for I have been an idle fellow all my life' " (I, 465).

On August 2, Boswell receives the great honor of being permitted to have tea with Miss Williams and on August 3 enjoys "our last social evening" at the Turk's Head. Johnson defends the notion of restoring the "Convocation to its full powers" (I, 464; to Boswell's surprise) and speaks of Colchester "with veneration, for having stood a siege for Charles the First" (I, 466). Boswell writes that Johnson "appeared to me *Jean Bull philosophe*" (I, 467-68); Johnson sends Boswell to his knees to ask divine protection in his journey. The passage as a whole is very representative. Johnson is thoroughly Boswellized. He is a high Anglican, high Tory, witty, social *Jean Bull*. In his own sphere his posture is royal:

My revered friend walked down with me to the beach, where we embraced and parted with tenderness, and engaged to correspond by letters. I said, "I hope, Sir, you will not forget me in my absence." JOHNSON. "Nay, Sir, it is more likely you should forget me, than that I should forget you." As the vessel put out to sea, I kept my eyes upon him for a considerable time, while he remained rolling his majestick frame in his usual manner: and at last I perceived him walk back into the town, and he disappeared. (I, 472)

The simplicity and economy of the passage is brilliant and given Boswell's personality Johnson's compliment is definitive. The world that awaits Boswell is kept in abeyance prior to his departure. At the moment of his departure, Johnson disappears into the town, epitomizing the transience of Boswell's joy and the manner in which the unique realm in which he has lived and moved may be quickly taken from him. In the very next paragraph (I, 473) Boswell's "spirits [are] grievously affected" and he is writing "a plaintive and desponding letter" to Johnson.

The craft in this passage is demonstrable. Boswell's own personality is illuminated throughout, while Johnson's is, in many ways, obscured. For the person seeking to understand Boswell the account of his departure and the events leading up to it is a garden; for the person seeking to understand Johnson it is a minefield. However, if these pages do not reveal Johnson in his complexity they do reveal what he was to Boswell and that, clearly, is a part of the total Johnson. What cannot be over-stressed is the fact that it is only a part.

In 1929 Andrew Macphail wrote of the *Life* that "any person of English speech, who has not read the book, is illiterate, without taste, without education, without interest in life" ("Johnson's Life of Boswell," p. 69), an aggressive judgment to be sure, but one which in its way is more acceptable than the common judgment repeated by Longaker that the *Life* is "the finest biography that the age—or that all time—produced" (*English Biography in the Eighteenth Century,* p. 407).

Measured against reasonable norms the *Life* falls far short as a biography; as an autobiographical document in which the autobiography is both conscious and unconscious it is very great indeed. Its success turns on the manner in which it is approached and the uses to which it is put.

A final point concerns the spirit in which we approach Boswell himself. I think it dangerous to patronize him. In an otherwise interesting article Leopold Damrosch describes Boswell in a fashion which I find troubling:

> In his ingenuous and childlike vanity, his fondness for festive occasions and for his own compositions in doggerel verse, and indeed in his capacity for loyal and demonstrative friendship, he perhaps reminds one of nobody so much as Toad of Toad Hall. (*"The Life of Johnson: An Anti-Theory,"* p. 502)

What we need (as always) is a balanced view of Boswell, one which avoids either patronizing him or damning him outright. He is certainly not above criticism. There is, for example, considerable justification for people like Lucas pointing to Boswell as a perpetual adolescent whose life was a series of amateur theatricals. The drinking, gambling, and womanizing, particularly in the later volumes of the Journal, are tedious and pathetic. The torturing of the mastiff which Paoli gave Boswell is both disgusting and reprehensible. (This is sometimes excused on the grounds that the age was a cruel one; Johnson's statements and personal practices in this regard suggest that the "age" had other alternatives.) In so many ways it is easy to feel sorry for Boswell, an emotion which nearly always leads to oversimplification, and of that, in the Boswell/Johnson relation, we have already had more than enough. Boswell is far less complex and far less interesting than Johnson but there is no reason to caricature him. He sacrificed and took great risks for some people just as he exploited others, and he suffered as much pain as he caused. He is a first-rate writer but one of very limited range. Johnson was essentially right when he complained that Boswell only had two subjects, but we have tired of neither.

BIBLIOGRAPHY
INDEX

Bibliography

BOSWELL AND JOHNSON,
PRIMARY SOURCES AND ABBREVIATIONS

Boswell's Life of Johnson. Edited by G. B. Hill. Revised and enlarged by
L. F. Powell. 6 vols. Oxford: Clarendon, 1934, 1950. (*Life*) (*Tour,*
V)

*The Private Papers of James Boswell from Malahide Castle in the
Collection of Lt.-Colonel Ralph Heyward Isham.* Edited by Geoffrey
Scott (I-VI) and Frederick A. Pottle (VII-XVIII). Mt. Vernon, N.Y.:
privately printed, 1928-34. (*PP*)

Boswell's London Journal, 1762-1763. Edited by Frederick A. Pottle.
New York: McGraw-Hill, 1950.

Boswell in Holland, 1763-1764. Edited by Frederick A. Pottle. New
York: McGraw-Hill, 1952.

Boswell on the Grand Tour: Germany and Switzerland, 1764. Edited
by Frederick A. Pottle. New York: McGraw-Hill, 1953.

Boswell on the Grand Tour: Italy, Corsica, and France, 1765-1766.
Edited by Frank Brady and Frederick A. Pottle. New York:
McGraw-Hill, 1955.

Boswell in Search of a Wife, 1766-1769. Edited by Frank Brady and
Frederick A. Pottle. New York: McGraw-Hill, 1956.

Boswell for the Defence, 1769-1774. Edited by William K. Wimsatt, Jr. and Frederick A. Pottle. New York: McGraw-Hill, 1959.

Boswell's Journal of a Tour to the Hebrides with Samuel Johnson, LL.D. Edited by Frederick A. Pottle and Charles H. Bennett. 2nd ed. New York: McGraw-Hill, 1961.

Boswell: The Ominous Years, 1774-1776. Edited by Charles Ryskamp and Frederick A. Pottle. New York: McGraw-Hill, 1963.

Boswell in Extremes, 1776-1778. Edited by Charles McC. Weis and Frederick A. Pottle. New York: McGraw-Hill, 1970.

The Correspondence of James Boswell and John Johnston of Grange. Edited by Ralph S. Walker. New York: McGraw-Hill, 1966. (*Corr—Grange*)

The Correspondence and Other Papers of James Boswell Relating to the Making of the "Life of Johnson." Edited by Marshall Waingrow. New York: McGraw-Hill, 1969. (*Corr—Life*)

The Correspondence of James Boswell with Certain Members of the Club. Edited by Charles N. Fifer. London: Heinemann, 1976. (*Corr—Club*)

Boswelliana: The Commonplace Book of James Boswell. Edited by Charles Rogers. London: Grampian Club, 1874.

Boswell, *The Hypochondriack.* Edited by Margery Bailey. 2 vols. Stanford: Stanford Univ. Press, 1928.

Samuel Johnson: A Journey to the Western Islands of Scotland. Edited by Mary Lascelles. New Haven: Yale Univ. Press, 1971.

Samuel Johnson: Diaries, Prayers, and Annals. Edited by E. L. McAdam, Jr., with Donald and Mary Hyde. New Haven: Yale Univ. Press, 1958.

Johnson on Shakespeare. Edited by Arthur Sherbo. 2 vols. New Haven: Yale Univ. Press, 1968.

Samuel Johnson: Life of Savage. Edited by Clarence Tracy. Oxford: Clarendon, 1971.

Samuel Johnson: Poems. Edited by E. L. McAdam, Jr., with George Milne. New Haven: Yale Univ. Press, 1964.

Samuel Johnson: The Idler and The Adventurer. Edited by W. J. Bate, John M. Bullitt, and L. F. Powell. New Haven: Yale Univ. Press, 1963.

Samuel Johnson: The Rambler. Edited by W. J. Bate and Albrecht B. Strauss. 3 vols. New Haven: Yale Univ. Press, 1969.

The Letters of Samuel Johnson: With Mrs. Thrale's Genuine Letters to Him. Edited by R. W. Chapman. 3 vols. Oxford: Clarendon, 1952.

The Works of Samuel Johnson, LL.D. 9 vols. Oxford, 1825. (*1825 Works*)

OTHER SOURCES, PRIMARY AND SECONDARY

Abrams, M. H. *Natural Supernaturalism: Tradition and Revolution in Romantic Literature.* New York: Norton, 1971.

Adams, Hazard. *The Interests of Criticism.* New York: Harcourt, Brace, 1969.

Alkon, Paul. "Boswellian Time." *Studies in Burke and His Time,* 14 (1973), 239-56.

_____. "Boswell's Control of Aesthetic Distance." *University of Toronto Quarterly,* 38 (1969), 174-91.

Altick, Richard D. *Lives and Letters: A History of Literary Biography in England and America.* New York: Knopf, 1965.

Amory, Hugh. "Boswell in Search of the Intentional Fallacy." *Bulletin of the New York Public Library,* 73 (1969), 24-39.

Ault, Donald D. *Visionary Physics: Blake's Response to Newton.* Chicago: Univ. of Chicago Press, 1974.

Bachelard, Gaston. *The Poetics of Space.* Translated by Maria Jolas. Boston: Beacon, 1969.

Balderston, Katharine C. "Johnson's Vile Melancholy." In *The Age of Johnson: Essays Presented to Chauncey Brewster Tinker,* edited by F. W. Hilles. New Haven: Yale Univ. Press, 1949.

Baldwin, Louis. "The Conversation in Boswell's *Life of Johnson.*" *Journal of English and Germanic Philology,* 51 (1952), 492-506.

Barker, John. *Strange Contrarieties: Pascal in England during the Age of Reason.* Montreal: McGill-Queen's Univ. Press, 1975.

Basney, Lionel. " 'Lucidus Ordo': Johnson and Generality." *Eighteenth-Century Studies,* 5 (1971), 39-57.

Bate, W. J. *The Achievement of Samuel Johnson.* New York: Oxford Univ. Press, 1955.

Bell, Robert H. "Boswell's Notes Toward a Supreme Fiction From *London Journal* to *Life of Johnson.*" *Modern Language Quarterly,* 38 (1977), 132-48.

Bloom, Edward A. "Johnson's 'Divided Self.' " *University of Toronto Quarterly,* 31 (1961), 42-53.

Bond, Donald F., ed. *The Spectator.* 5 vols. Oxford: Clarendon, 1965.

Boulton, James T., ed. *Johnson: The Critical Heritage.* New York: Barnes & Noble, 1971.

Brack, O M, Jr. and Robert E. Kelley, eds. *The Early Biographies of Samuel Johnson.* Iowa City: Univ. of Iowa Press, 1974.

Bracken, Harry M. *The Early Reception of Berkeley's Immaterialism, 1710-1733.* The Hague: Nijhoff, 1959.

Brady, Frank. "Boswell's Self-Presentation and His Critics." *Studies in English Literature*, 12 (1972), 545-55.

Braudy, Leo. "Lexicography and Biography in the *Preface* to Johnson's *Dictionary.*" *Studies in English Literature*, 10 (1970), 551-56.

Britt, Albert. *The Great Biographers.* New York: McGraw-Hill, 1936.

Bronson, Bertrand Harris. *Facets of the Enlightenment: Studies in English Literature and Its Contexts.* Berkeley and Los Angeles: Univ. of California Press, 1968.

_____. *Johnson Agonistes and Other Essays.* Berkeley and Los Angeles: Univ. of California Press, 1965.

Brooks, A. Russell. *James Boswell.* New York: Twayne, 1971.

Bruss, Elizabeth W. *Autobiographical Acts: The Changing Situation of a Literary Genre.* Baltimore: The Johns Hopkins Univ. Press, 1976.

Buchdahl, Gerd. *The Image of Newton and Locke in the Age of Reason.* London: Sheed & Ward, 1961.

Butt, John. *Biography in the Hands of Walton, Johnson, and Boswell.* Los Angeles: UCLA, 1966 (the Ewing lectures).

Carlyle, Thomas. *On Heroes and Hero-Worship.* London: Fraser, 1841.

_____. [Review of Croker]. *Fraser's Magazine*, 5 (1832), 379-413.

Carr, Edward Hallett. *What is History?* New York: Vintage, 1961.

Cassirer, Ernst. *An Essay on Man: An Introduction to a Philosophy of Human Culture.* 1944; Reprinted New York: Bantam, 1970.

Catford, E. F. *Edinburgh: The Story of A City.* London: Hutchinson, 1975.

Chapin, Chester F. "Johnson and Pascal." In *English Writers of the Eighteenth Century*, edited by John H. Middendorf. New York: Columbia Univ. Press, 1971.

Chapman, R. W., ed. *Boswell's Note Book, 1776-1777, Recording Particulars of Johnson's Early Life Communicated by Him and Others in Those Years.* London: Milford, 1925.

_____. "Boswell's Proof-Sheets." *London Mercury*, 15 (1926), 50-58, 171-80.

Clifford, James L., ed. *Biography as an Art: Selected Criticism, 1560-1960.* New York: Oxford Univ. Press, 1962.

_____. "How Much Should a Biographer Tell? Some Eighteenth-Century Views." In *Essays In Eighteenth-Century Biography*, edited by Philip B. Daghlian. Bloomington: Indiana Univ. Press, 1968.

_____. "Some Aspects of London Life in the Mid-18th Century." In *City & Society in the 18th Century*, edited by Paul Fritz and David Williams. Toronto: Hakkert, 1973.

_____. *Young Sam Johnson*. New York: McGraw-Hill, 1955.

Cohen, I. Bernard. *Franklin and Newton: An Inquiry into Speculative Newtonian Experimental Science and Franklin's Work in Electricity as an Example Thereof*. Cambridge: Harvard Univ. Press, 1966.

Coleman, William H. "The Johnsonian Conversational Formula." *Quarterly Review*, 282 (1944), 432-45.

Collins, P. A. W. "Boswell's Contact with Johnson." *Notes and Queries*, 201 (1956), 163-66.

Damrosch, Leopold, Jr. "*The Life of Johnson*: An Anti-Theory." *Eighteenth-Century Studies*, 6 (1973), 486-505.

Davis, Herbert. "The Augustan Conception of History." In *Reason and the Imagination: Studies in the History of Ideas, 1600-1800*, edited by J. A. Mazzeo. New York: Columbia Univ. Press, 1962.

Davis, John W. "Berkeley, Newton, and Space." In *The Methodological Heritage of Newton*, edited by Robert E. Butts and John W. Davis. Toronto: Univ. of Toronto Press, 1970.

Dowling, William C. "The Boswellian Hero." *Studies in Scottish Literature*, 10 (1972), 79-93.

Drinkwater, John. *The Muse in Council*. London: Sidgwick and Jackson, 1925.

Dunne, John S. *A Search for God in Time and Memory*. New York: Macmillan, 1967.

_____. *The City of the Gods: A Study in Myth and Mortality*. New York: Macmillan, 1965.

_____. *The Way of All the Earth: Experiments in Truth and Religion*. New York: Macmillan, 1972.

Eckermann, Johann Peter. *Words of Goethe: Being the Conversations of Johann Wolfgang von Goethe*. New York: Tudor, 1949.

Elder, A. T. "Irony and Humour in the *Rambler*." *University of Toronto Quarterly*, 30 (1960), 57-71.

Evans, Bergen B. "Dr. Johnson's Theory of Biography." *Review of English Studies*, 10 (1934), 301-10.

Fitzgerald, Percy. *Boswell's Autobiography*. London: Chatto & Windus, 1912.

Frye, Northrop. *Fables of Identity: Studies in Poetic Mythology*. New York: Harcourt, Brace, 1963.

_____. *The Stubborn Structure: Essays on Criticism and Society*. Ithaca: Cornell Univ. Press, 1970.

Folkenflik, Robert. "Johnson's Art of Anecdote." In *Racism in the Eighteenth Century*, edited by Harold E. Pagliaro. Studies in Eighteenth-Century Culture, vol. 3. Cleveland: Case Western Reserve Press, 1953.

Fussell, Paul, Jr. "The Force of Literary Memory in Boswell's *London Journal.*" *Studies in English Literature,* 2 (1962), 351-57.

———. "The Memorable Scenes of Mr. Boswell." *Encounter,* 28 (1967), 70-77.

Garraty, John A. *The Nature of Biography.* New York: Knopf, 1957.

Goethe. *The Autobiography of Johann Wolfgang von Goethe.* Translated by John Oxenford, introduced by Karl J. Weintraub. 2 vols. Chicago: Univ. of Chicago Press, 1974.

Greene, Donald J. "Reflections on a Literary Anniversary." *Queen's Quarterly,* 70 (1963), 198-208.

———. "Samuel Johnson and 'Natural Law.'" *Journal of British Studies,* 2 (1963), 59-75, 84-87.

———. *Samuel Johnson's Library: An Annotated Guide.* English Literary Studies, University of Victoria, vol. 1. Victoria, B.C., 1975.

———. "Smart, Berkeley, the Scientists and the Poets: A Note on Eighteenth-Century Anti-Newtonianism." *Journal of the History of Ideas,* 14 (1953), 327-52.

———. "The Making of Boswell's Life of Johnson." *Studies in Burke and His Time,* 12 (1970-71), 1812-20.

———. *The Politics of Samuel Johnson.* New Haven: Yale Univ. Press, 1960.

———. "The Uses of Autobiography in the Eighteenth Century." In *Essays in Eighteenth-Century Biography,* edited by Philip B. Daghlian. Bloomington: Indiana Univ. Press, 1968.

———. "'Tis a Pretty Book, Mr. Boswell, But—." Unpublished paper.

Grinnell, George. "Newton's *Principia* as Whig Propaganda." In *City and Society in the 18th Century,* edited by Paul Fritz and David Williams. Toronto: Hakkert, 1973.

Guerlac, Henry. "Where the Statue Stood: Divergent Loyalties to Newton in the Eighteenth Century." In *Aspects of the Eighteenth Century,* edited by Earl R. Wasserman. Baltimore: The Johns Hopkins Press, 1965.

Hagstrum, Jean H. *The Sister Arts: The Tradition of Literary Pictorialism and English Poetry from Dryden to Gray.* Chicago: Univ. of Chicago Press, 1958.

Haller, William. *The Rise of Puritanism.* New York: Columbia Univ. Press, 1938.

Hart, Francis R. "Boswell and the Romantics: A Chapter in the History of Biographical Theory." *ELH,* 27 (1960), 44-65.

Hawkins, Sir John. *The Life of Samuel Johnson, LL.D.* 2nd ed. London, 1787.

Hirsch, E. D., Jr. *Validity in Interpretation.* New Haven: Yale Univ. Press, 1967.

Howarth, William L. "Some Principles of Autobiography." *New Literary History,* 5 (1974), 363-81.

Hume, David. *An Inquiry Concerning Human Understanding.* Edited by Charles W. Hendel. New York: Liberal Arts Press, 1955.

_____. *A Treatise of Human Nature.* Edited by Ernest C. Mossner. Baltimore: Penguin, 1969.

_____. *Of the Standard of Taste and Other Essays.* Edited by John W. Lenz. Indianapolis: Bobbs-Merrill, 1965.

Irwin, M. G. "Dr. Johnson's Troubled Mind." *Literature and Psychology,* 13 (1963), 6-11.

_____. *Samuel Johnson: A Personality in Conflict.* Auckland: Auckland Univ. Press, 1971.

Jack, Ian. "Two Biographers: Lockhart and Boswell." In *Johnson, Boswell and their Circle: Essays Presented to Lawrence Fitzroy Powell in Honour of His Eighty-fourth Birthday,* edited by Mary M. Lascelles et al. Oxford: Clarendon, 1965.

Jung, C. G. *Memories, Dreams, Reflections.* Edited by Aniela Jaffé, translated by Richard and Clara Winston. Rev. ed. New York: Vintage, 1963.

_____. *Modern Man in Search of a Soul.* Translated by W. S. Dell and Cary F. Baynes. New York: Harcourt, Brace, n.d. (orig. publ. 1933).

Kant, Immanuel. *Critique of Pure Reason.* Translated by Max Müller. Garden City: Doubleday, 1966.

Kennet, Basil, trans. *Thoughts on Religion, and other Curious Subjects, Written Originally in French by Monsieur Pascal.* 2nd ed. London, 1727.

Kermode, Frank. *The Sense of an Ending: Studies in the Theory of Fiction.* London: Oxford Univ. Press, 1967.

Kiley, Frederick S. "Boswell's Literary Art in the *London Journal.*" *College English,* 23 (1962), 629-32.

Korshin, Paul J. "*Ana*-Books and Intellectual Biography in the Eighteenth Century." In *Racism in the Eighteenth Century,* edited by Harold E. Pagliaro. Studies in Eighteenth-Century Culture, vol. 3. Cleveland: Case Western Reserve Press, 1973.

_____. "An Unrecovered World: Samuel Parr's Projected Life of Johnson." Unpublished paper presented at Modern Language Association convention, 1971.

_____. "Dr. Johnson and Jeremy Bentham: An Unnoticed Relationship." *Modern Philology,* 70 (1972/1973), 38-45.

Krutch, Joseph Wood. "On the Talk of Samuel Johnson and his Friends." *American Scholar*, 13 (1944), 263-72.

_____. *Samuel Johnson*. 1944; Reprinted New York: Harcourt, Brace, 1963.

Lane, Margaret. *Samuel Johnson & His World*. London: Hamish Hamilton, 1976.

Laudan, L. L. "Thomas Reid and the Newtonian Turn of British Methodological Thought." In *The Methodological Heritage of Newton*, edited by Robert E. Butts and John W. Davis. Toronto: Univ. of Toronto Press, 1970.

Letwin, Shirley Robin. *The Pursuit of Certainty: David Hume, Jeremy Bentham, John Stuart Mill, Beatrice Webb*. Cambridge: Cambridge Univ. Press, 1965.

Lipking, Lawrence. "Art, Morals, Madness: Some Problems in Writing the Lives of Pope, Johnson, and Blake." Unpublished paper presented at Modern Language Association convention, 1975.

Longaker, Mark. *English Biography in the Eighteenth Century*. Philadelphia: Univ. of Pennsylvania Press, 1931.

Lonsdale, Roger. "Dr. Burney and the Integrity of Boswell's Quotations." *Papers of the Bibliographical Society of America*, 53 (1959), 327-31.

Lucas, F. L. *Literature and Psychology*. Rev. ed. Ann Arbor: Univ. of Michigan Press, 1957.

_____. *The Search for Good Sense: Four Eighteenth-Century Characters*. London: Cassell, 1958.

Lustig, Irma S. "Boswell on Politics in *The Life of Johnson*." *PMLA*, 80 (1965), 387-93.

_____. "Boswell's Literary Criticism in *The Life of Johnson*." *Studies in English Literature*, 6 (1966), 529-41.

_____. "Boswell's Portrait of Himself in *The Life of Samuel Johnson*." Diss. Pennsylvania 1963.

Macaulay, Thomas Babington. "Boswell's Life of Johnson." *Edinburgh Review*, 54 (1831), 1-38.

McAdam, E. L., Jr. *Johnson & Boswell: A Survey of Their Writings*. Boston: Houghton Mifflin, 1969.

McConnell, Frank D. *The Confessional Imagination: A Reading of Wordsworth's "Prelude."* Baltimore: The Johns Hopkins Univ. Press, 1974.

Macphail, Andrew. "Johnson's Life of Boswell." *Quarterly Review*, 253 (1929), 42-73.

Mallory, George. *Boswell the Biographer.* London: Smith, Elder & Co., 1912.

Molin, Sven Eric. "Boswell's Account of the Johnson-Wilkes Meeting." *Studies in English Literature,* 3 (1963), 307-22.

Morris, John N. *Versions of the Self: Studies in English Autobiography from John Bunyan to John Stuart Mill.* New York: Basic Books, 1966.

Newton, Isaac. *Opticks: or a Treatise of the Reflections, Refractions, Inflections & Colours of Light.* New York: Dover, 1952.

Olney, James. *Metaphors of Self: The Meaning of Autobiography.* Princeton: Princeton Univ. Press, 1972.

Pascal, Blaise. *Pascal's Pensées.* Translated by H. F. Stewart. New York: Modern Library, n.d.

Pascal, Roy. *Design and Truth in Autobiography.* London: Routledge & Kegan Paul, 1960.

Passler, David L. *Time, Form, and Style in Boswell's "Life of Johnson."* New Haven: Yale Univ. Press, 1971.

Paulson, Ronald. *Hogarth: His Life, Art, and Times.* 2 vols. New Haven: Yale Univ. Press, 1971.

Phillipson, Nicholas. "Towards a Definition of the Scottish Enlightenment." In *City and Society in the 18th Century,* edited by Paul Fritz and David Williams. Toronto: Hakkert, 1973.

Piozzi, Hester Lynch Thrale. *Anecdotes of the Late Samuel Johnson, LL.D.* In vol. I of *Johnsonian Miscellanies,* edited by G. B. Hill. Oxford: Clarendon, 1897.

Plato, *Timaeus and Critias.* Translated by H. D. P. Lee. Harmondsworth: Penguin, 1971.

Popkin, Richard H. "David Hume: His Pyrrhonism and His Critique of Pyrrhonism." In *Hume,* edited by V. C. Chappell. Garden City: Doubleday, 1966.

_____. *The History of Scepticism from Erasmus to Descartes.* Rev. ed. New York: Harper & Row, 1968.

Pottle, Frederick A. "Boswell Revalued." In *Literary Views: Critical and Historical Essays,* edited by Carroll Camden. Rice Univ. Semicentennial Publications, Chicago: Univ. of Chicago Press, 1964.

_____. "Boswell's University Education." In *Johnson, Boswell and their Circle: Essays Presented to Lawrence Fitzroy Powell in Honour of His Eighty-fourth Birthday,* edited by Mary M. Lascelles et al. Oxford: Clarendon, 1965.

_____. "James Boswell, Journalist." In *The Age of Johnson: Essays Presented to Chauncey Brewster Tinker*, edited by Frederick W. Hilles. New Haven: Yale Univ. Press, 1949.

_____. *James Boswell, the Earlier Years: 1740-1769.* New York: McGraw-Hill, 1966.

_____. "The Dark Hints of Sir John Hawkins and Boswell." In *New Light on Dr. Johnson: Essays on the Occasion of his 250th Birthday*, edited by F. W. Hilles. New Haven: Yale Univ. Press, 1959.

_____. "The Life of Boswell." *Yale Review*, 35 (1946), 445-60.

_____. "The Life of Johnson: Art and Authenticity." In *Twentieth-Century Interpretations of Boswell's "Life of Johnson": A Collection of Critical Essays*, edited by James L. Clifford. Englewood Cliffs: Prentice-Hall, 1970.

_____. *The Literary Career of James Boswell, Esq., Being the Bibliographical Materials for a Life of Boswell.* Oxford: Clarendon, 1929.

_____. "The Power of Memory in Boswell and Scott." In *Essays on the Eighteenth Century Presented to David Nichol Smith.* Oxford: Clarendon, 1945.

Priestley, F. E. L. "Newton and the Romantic Concept of Nature." *University of Toronto Quarterly*, 17 (1948), 323-36.

Priestley, J. B. *Man and Time.* New York: Dell, 1964.

Primeau, Ronald. "Boswell's 'Romantic Imagination' in the *London Journal."* *Papers on Language and Literature*, 9 (1973), 15-27.

Quinlan, Maurice. "Dr. Franklin Meets Dr. Johnson." *Pennsylvania Magazine of History and Biography*, 73 (1949), 34-44.

_____. *Samuel Johnson: A Layman's Religion.* Madison: Univ. of Wisconsin Press, 1964.

Rader, Ralph W. "Literary Form in Factual Narrative: The Example of Boswell's *Johnson."* In *Essays In Eighteenth-Century Biography*, edited by Philip B. Daghlian. Bloomington: Indiana Univ. Press, 1968.

Randall, John Herman Jr. "Newton's Natural Philosophy: Its Problems and Consequences." In *Philosophical Essays in Honor of Edgar Arthur Singer, Jr.*, edited by F. P. Clarke and M. C. Nahm. Philadelphia: Univ. of Pennsylvania Press, 1942.

Reid, B. L. "Johnson's Life of Boswell." *Kenyon Review*, 18 (1956), 546-75.

Richmond, Hugh M. "Personal Identity and Literary Personae: A Study in Historical Psychology." *PMLA*, 90 (1975), 209-21.

Rosenbaum, S. P., ed. *English Literature and British Philosophy.* Chicago: Univ. of Chicago Press, 1971.

Ross, Ian. "Boswell in Search of a Father? or a Subject?" *Review of English Literature*, 5 (1964), 19-34.

Rothstein, Eric. " 'Ideal Presence' and the 'Non Finito' in Eighteenth-Century Aesthetics." *Eighteenth-Century Studies*, 9 (1976), 307-32.

_____. *Systems of Order and Inquiry in Later Eighteenth-Century Fiction*. Berkeley and Los Angeles: Univ. of California Press, 1975.

Rudé, George. *Hanoverian London, 1714-1808*. Berkeley and Los Angeles: Univ. of California Press, 1971.

Saintsbury, George. *The Collected Essays and Papers, 1875-1920*. Vol. I. London: Dent, 1923.

Scott, Geoffrey. *The Making of the Life of Johnson as Shown in Boswell's First Notes, Original Diaries, and Revised Drafts: A Study of Boswell's Biographical Method Marking the Successive Steps in the Composition* (*Private Papers*, VI, 1929).

Shaftesbury, Anthony Ashley Cooper. 3rd Earl of. *Characteristics of Men, Manners, Opinions, Times*. Edited by John M. Robertson. Indianapolis: Bobbs-Merrill, 1964.

Siebenschuh, William R. *Form and Purpose in Boswell's Biographical Works*. Berkeley and Los Angeles: Univ. of California Press, 1972.

_____. "The Relationship between Factual Accuracy and Literary Art in the *Life of Johnson*." *Modern Philology*, 74 (1977), 273-88.

Silver, Bruce Sheldon. "The Status of the Sciences in the Philosophy of George Berkeley." Diss. Colorado 1971.

Smollett, Tobias. *The Adventures of Peregrine Pickle, in which are included Memoirs of a Lady of Quality*. Edited by James L. Clifford. London: Oxford Univ. Press, 1964.

Stauffer, Donald A. *English Biography before 1700*. Cambridge: Harvard Univ. Press, 1930.

_____. *The Art of Biography in Eighteenth-Century England*. 2 vols. Princeton: Princeton Univ. Press, 1941.

Sterne, Laurence. *The Life and Opinions of Tristram Shandy, Gentleman*. Edited by James Aiken Work. New York: Odyssey, 1940.

Stock, R. D. *Samuel Johnson and Neoclassical Dramatic Theory: The Intellectual Context of the Preface to Shakespeare*. Lincoln: Univ. of Nebraska Press, 1973.

Strachey, Lytton. "James Boswell." *The Nation & The Athenaeum*, Jan. 31, 1925, pp. 609-10.

Taylor, Frank. "Johnsoniana from the Bagshawe Muniments in the John Rylands Library: Sir James Caldwell, Dr. Hawkesworth, Dr. Johnson, and Boswell's Use of the 'Caldwell Minute.' " *Bulletin of the John Rylands Library*, 35 (1952), 211-47.

Thayer, H. S., ed. *Newton's Philosophy of Nature*. Introduction by John Herman Randall, Jr. New York: Hafner, 1953.

Tillinghast, Anthony J. "The Moral and Philosophical Basis of Johnson's and Boswell's Idea of Biography." In *Johnsonian Studies*, edited by Magdi Wahba. Cairo: privately printed, 1962.

Tinker, Chauncey Brewster. *The Salon and English Letters: Chapters on the Interrelations of Literature and Society in the Age of Johnson*. New York: Macmillan, 1915.

_____. *Young Boswell*. Boston: The Atlantic Monthly Press, 1922.

Todd, William B. "Cowper's Commentary on the *Life of Johnson*." *Times Literary Supplement*, March 15, 1957, p. 168.

Toulmin, Stephen and June Goodfield. *The Discovery of Time*. London: Hutchinson, 1965.

Tracy, Clarence. "Boswell: The Cautious Empiricist." In *The Triumph of Culture: 18th-Century Perspectives*, edited by Paul Fritz and David Williams. Toronto: Hakkert, 1972.

_____. "Johnson and the Art of Anecdote." *University of Toronto Quarterly*, 15 (1945), 86-93.

Trowbridge, Hoyt. "Scattered Atoms of Probability." *Eighteenth-Century Studies*, 5 (1971), 1-38.

Van Doren, Mark, ed. *The New Invitation to Learning*. New York: Random House, 1942 (dialogue on *Life* by Isham, Krutch, Van Doren, pp. 283-96).

Van Leeuwen, Henry G. *The Problem of Certainty in English Thought, 1630-1690*. The Hague: Nijhoff, 1963.

Verbeek, E. *The Measure and the Choice: A Pathographic Essay on Samuel Johnson*. Ghent: E. Story-Scientia, 1971.

Voitle, Robert. *Samuel Johnson the Moralist*. Cambridge: Harvard Univ. Press, 1961.

Voltaire. *Philosophical Letters*. Translated by Ernest Dilworth. Indianapolis: Bobbs-Merrill, 1961.

Wain, John, ed. *Johnson as Critic*. London: Routledge & Kegan Paul, 1973.

_____. *Johnson on Johnson*. New York: Dutton, 1976.

_____. *Samuel Johnson*. New York: Viking, 1975.

_____. *Samuel Johnson: Lives of the English Poets, A Selection*. London: Dent, 1975.

Ward, John Chapman. "Johnson's Conversation." *Studies in English Literature*, 12 (1972), 519-33.

Wasserman, Earl R. "Nature Moralized: The Divine Analogy in the Eighteenth Century." *ELH*, 20 (1953), 39-76.

Weinbrot, Howard D. "Samuel Johnson's *Plan* and Preface to the Dictionary: The Growth of a Lexicographer's Mind." In *New Aspects of Lexicography: Literary Criticism, Intellectual History, and Social Change,* edited by Howard D. Weinbrot. Carbondale: Southern Illinois Univ. Press, 1972.

Werkmeister, Lucyle. *Jemmie Boswell and the London Daily Press, 1785-1795.* New York: The New York Public Library, 1963.

Wilde, Oscar. "The Decay of Lying." In *Critical Theory Since Plato,* edited by Hazard Adams. New York: Harcourt Brace, 1971.

Wilson, F. P. "Table Talk." *Huntington Library Quarterly,* 4 (1940), 27-46.

Wimsatt, W. K. "Images of Samuel Johnson." *ELH,* 41 (1974), 359-74.

_____. "The Fact Imagined: James Boswell." In *Hateful Contraries: Studies in Literature and Criticism.* Lexington: Univ. of Kentucky Press, 1965.

Wittgenstein, Ludwig. *On Certainty.* Edited by G. E. M. Anscombe and G. H. von Wright, translated by Denis Paul and G. E. M. Anscombe. New York: Harper & Row, 1972.

Note: W. Jackson Bate's *Samuel Johnson* appeared after my study was completed. For comments on Bate's biography see my review in *The Georgia Review,* 32 (1978), 217-21.

Index

Abrams, M. H., 85
Adams, William, 56
Addison, Joseph, 4, 40, 82
Alkon, Paul, xiii, 15-16, 18, 28, 39*n*, 72*n*, 95-96
Amory, Hugh, 20
"Artistic" biography, 8-9
Art/life distinction. *See* Life/art distinction
Aubrey, John, 4
Auchinleck, Alexander Boswell, Lord, 52-53

Bachelard, Gaston, 38
Bacon, Francis, 4, 17, 31, 33
Banks, Sir Joseph, 101
Barker, John, 84*n*, 85 and *n*
Barnard, Frederick, 51
Bate, W. Jackson, 121
Bayle, Pierre, 61
Beauclerk, Topham, 101

Berkeley, George: and scientific method, 32; criticism of Newtonian absolutes and "certainty," 32-33; and Baconian utility, 33; denial of primary/secondary qualities distinction, 35; and human valuation, 40
Blair, Hugh, 17-18
Blake, William, 86, 89
Bolton, Charles Paulet, 3rd Duke of, 41
Boswell, James: *London Journal*, xii, 32, 44-47, 65-68, 89; and SJ's biographical theory, 3; image of SJ, 10, 25-27; biographical art and "authenticity," 11-18; time spent with SJ, 13; theory of biography not defined, 15; metaphors for *Life*, 15-18; arrangement of materials in *Life*, 18; knowledge of science, 20; SJ-Wilkes meeting, 20, 44, 48, 53,

COMPOSED BY FOX VALLEY TYPESETTING, MENASHA, WISCONSIN
MANUFACTURED BY THOMSON-SHORE, INC., DEXTER, MICHIGAN
TEXT AND DISPLAY ARE SET IN PALATINO

ᵾ

Library of Congress Cataloging in Publication Data
Schwartz, Richard B.
Boswell's Johnson: a preface to the Life.
Bibliography: p.
Includes index.
1. Boswell, James, 1740-1795.
Life of Samuel Johnson. 2. Johnson,
Samuel, 1709-1784—Biography. 3. Authors,
English—18th century—Biography. 4. Biography (as a literary
form) I. Title.
PR3533.B7S3   828'.6'09 [B]   78-4509
ISBN 0-299-07630-X